MW01516620

In What Furnace?

POEMS BY

Teresa White

Two Steps Publishing Co.

Two Steps Publishing Company – October 1997
Copyright ©1997 by Teresa White

All rights reserved under international and
Pan American copyright conventions. Published in
the United States by TWO STEPS PUBLISHING CO.
A division of THE BLAKE GROUP–San Francisco, CA

Library of Congress Cataloging-in-publication Data

White, Teresa, 1947
IN WHAT FURNACE / Teresa White
First TWO STEPS PUBLISHING CO. edition
1996 Louis Road, Palo Alto, CA 94303

p. cm.- (In What Furnace)

ISBN 0-9640223-0-3

I. Title II. Series

Library of Congress Catalog Card Number   94-60022
CIP
Book Design by Valerie Reichert
Manufactured in the United States of America
10 9 8 7 6 5 4

To my loving husband,
Rob

What the hammer? What the chain?
In what furnace was thy brain?
What the anvil? what dread grasp
Dare its deadly terrors clasp?

William Blake (The Tyger)

In What Furnace?

Embryonic Memory

Now, while feeling birth
tight, tighter, tight...

A scream from my mother;
beauty abounds.

...Remembering stillness,
there's a white room and me.

As We Are Born

Some are born beautiful.
They must spend their lives
proving their intelligence.

Some are born homely.
They must spend their lives
building their character.

Some are born ignorant.
They must spend their lives
laughing at bad jokes.

Some are born brilliant.
They must spend their lives
seeking answers.

Some are born wise.
They must spend their lives
teaching us all
to accept ourselves as we are.

Writing

a poem is like painting a picture.
First...gather your supplies.
Then, sit in a good northern light.

You will need an idea,
A page white as gesso,
A palette of words:
> prismatic nouns
> garish verbs
> stunning adjectives.

Your words should shimmer on the page
like cerulean blue
in a Van Gogh night sky.
They should be well-oiled as linseed,
nubile as pale rose,
important as green.

Your poem should use fine strokes
in the telling...but be wary of
overwork

for the skin of truth is delicate
as rice paper
floating
on a pool of water.

When I Consider My Writing Life

I feel like Joan of Arc must have felt imagining
her own death
as the flames licked at her
feet.

Words fail me like a flame
built to put out a forest fire but which
only makes it worse.

I write with a tambourine in my hand
in this scaffold square of madness just under the
surface of the waking me...

or, I am Hugos's Esmeralda
tapping my small white feet
in a dance
to earn my keep

or, I am a drowning victim
gulping for air who has to decide
should she take the last deep breath of air
or
risk all
and call for help.

Letters

You tell me of the hummingbirds
I tell you of the rain
And every other word we've said
We say it once again.

But when the hummingbirds are gone
And the rain has turned to sun,
You'll tell me of your reading
class.
I'll tell of chrysanthemums.

The letters tick the years away,
recording birds and flowers,
Our lives are forged by Hallmark
described in greeting cards.

The hummingbirds flash quick and
pink
And blur into a song–

I love you Mother, the years go
by,
Our lives are lived… go on.

No biographers

I'll have no biographers
twenty years from now
telling tales into a microphone
or paper cup full of memories...
full of achievements secured
astraddle rush-hour traffic traveling
homeward.

You could say Grecian urns lie in pieces
at my feet
from abuse or neglect I cannot say
It's just they didn't suit the light
arriving in a VanDyke sort of way
or filtered through my husband's Kodak
on a conspicuous, serene sort of day.

Survival of the fittest
the phrase is punched up on my screen of long term
memory.
Stainless steel lungs
perhaps would be useful or the stamina of
a hummingbird in flight
feeding on quince or buttercup
beside the sluggish river.

The Rainbow

I ran & ran trying to reach
the end of the rainbow
before it faded
I ran out of the house in the pouring rain
without any coat

My hair stuck to my frozen cheek
like seaweed
I ran through the mud which
speckled my legs

I ran & ran gasping for breath
goaded with greed
for the pot of gold
the rainbow's gift for those who believe

Stumbling,
 I reached the rainbow's end
and nothing was there
        nothing was there
Nothing was there but the end of the road
and the wind

which I swear I could hear laughing.

Sleepwalk

The night was warm and smelled of musty camping
outings.
She always slept cocooned in an old sleeping bag
The warmth fell away as her toes pressed quietly
upon the slatted wood of her bedroom floor.

The bathroom was clear downstairs. A long way
to guess the path of darkness.
Discovering the top railing, her long hand
traced the wooden curve while her foot swayed
through the black-curtained air
hunting for the first step.

She thought she would cut down on her coffee
so this wouldn't be necessary every night.
The bathroom was small as a tomb and the windows were
cold.

It wasn't so much the entering she minded but
rather not knowing– or understanding–
what might be waiting for her
in the hallway
or back up in her room.

Return

The felt-tongued caterpillar stares at me
Alone in my room which never grows old.
Every day I am different and walk into
The fading familiarity of my jewelled house.
These self-portraits mock me from the walls,
These books dare me to read them a second time,
My candles never stop melting.

Adagio

effort   less
ly
they glide through the air

per   fect
ly
their bodies are a pair

linked muscle to sinew
in composition
no painter can repeat

their feet
are fluttering birds
beat-ing wing to wing in mid-air

Hold your breath,
for they will soar so high & light . . .

and then be gone

Unchained Posey

Man reach out for woman
Woman reach out for man
The sun reach for children
The moon reach for civilization

Hiawatha dance in heaven
He dance for evermore
His land of skyblue waters
Is tide on every shore

This body deny the tide
That man hate his shore
Woman sing her child to sleep
Child love his mother's song

Growing

We grow and grow
playing mommy in the
lipsticked mirror–
hoping for a true reflection
that hides behind
a truthful smear.

Metamorphosis

A seed, after love, divided and grew
then opened and became me.
I grew slowly at first– slowly
I was aware of the world
pulsing in rooms other than mine.
I moved into an era of waxed
linoleum floors upon which
people were above me, or stooped
down to me– teaching me to
dry spoons and keep myself clean.
The momentous days spun fast and strong
kind enough to give me an occasional
glimpse at Hans Christian Anderson
and candy-filled paper trains
at Christmas.
My cocoon of youth slipped away
in those twirling days when
I wasn't looking
And now flapping I race
the tumbler of time,
becoming adult,
as the funnel of the past
gushes me out.

Lie For A Daughter

The lie I heard from childhood
was my mother's promise to me.

You'll be a woman someday
and speak words as sure as
butter melting on a summer table.

Children will rustle in your skirts,
your hair will favor the shape
of your neck,
your laughter will be soft and song-like.

Your body will be ample and soft
under goosedown coverlets.

Mother's Day Poem

I feel close to you as a sister
I feel close, beloved Mother
To you who loves your daughter
For this, my heart is joyful

For this, my heart is joyful
And I shall love you ever

Poem on My Twenty-Ninth Birthday

Almost thirty
Nearer forty
Gone is sixteen
Soon I'm fifty.

Once I wore my skin-tight sweaters
To catch the grocery-checker's eye
To flirt & make-out for one-night
Stands, a little weed, low-lights,
Bob Dylan.

Now it's beer in front of t.v.
Wearing married smiles & clothes.
Now it's hard to be a beauty
Though the inside's just as wild.

Almost thirty
Nearer forty
Gone is sixteen
Soon I'm fifty.

At The Grocery Store

In my quiet & ticking breast
Lives a girl no longer young
While the pretty people jest
She just stands and watches them

Housewife hands with dimestore polish
Crowsfeet eyes with silver cream
She feels alone and insular
In the grocery check-out line.

Visiting Hours

We enter the trim parking lot
turn the car's motor off between
white parallel designatory lines and begin
our eagerly awaited but grim walk toward
the generous entrance.

Natural wood-stained glass-paneled doors
swing inward as we enter the pastel reception area.
Pink & silver striped facsimiles of Louis 14th settees
line the walls...
Mary Cassatt paintings celebrate motherhood and youth.

She could do worse
I think as my husband and I advance down the
carpeted hallway nodding polite and remote smiles
to wheelchair-strapped residents recreating in the
lonesome halls.

Hand-crocheted afghans hide arthritic knees and it
seems as if the men's and women's heads are suddenly
too large for their bodies and that they sag downward
toward empty laps.

Gravity and sons and daughters have done this I think.

Hispanic aides– robust and efficient– numerate the
rooms with their unselfconscious laughter and foreign
jokes.
We round the endless concourse past a nurses' station

18

redolent with rubbing alcohol and metallic clipboards.

Sharply, we hear the cry of a parrot or monkey.
We glance at the beaten faces but see no lips move.

God, age is unkind to man
I realize
as I catch a scent of floor wax and overripe fruit.

A few more rooms;
a few more doorways and we'll see our friend.

She is glancing downwards.
She is strapped to her wheelchair.
She will be all alone when we leave.

Schoolchildren

In October
red-leaved promises
slump homeward on the
muddy shoes of school children

who would be luckier
if they
knew how young they were.

At night,
Sleep leaves a soft imprint of death
upon their cheeks,
now a bright pink in the cool air.

They walk from here to there,
hunched down a concrete trail,
with their parents' dreams
rattling
in their empty lunch pails.

Before I Die

1.

Before I die
I want to know that life will go on

I want butterflies to mate
amidst enviable green camouflage;
Trout to spawn in cool blue streams
going on & on & on.

I want pine & fir trees to reach the sky
and leave a carpet of lush needles for
my path in the oh so certain woods

I want to know I can rely on what has been good:
the comforting 'Rockwell' family sitting
down to Sunday Chicken
the kids struggling with school
Dad catching a big one on a fishing weekend…

Before I die
I want to see another hill,
another promise to keep or challenge
to meet

I'd like to know the other side has
someone just like me

Deciding to go or stay.

2.

Television sets are warm in America's
living rooms
as we forsake our supper
and listen to one more scientist explain
the death of our planet.

from neglect
from misuse
from a direct hit...

Before I die
I want to know I'll be buried
in that pretty green cemetary on the hill
and that when you come visit me

the flowers that you place upon my grave
will be real
and that the grave
will always be there.

The Change

We learn dignity
as we praise the gray hairs
the double chins

Why are we kidding
ourselves into thinking
that our mirrors don't lie?

Come now, just how far
can we go with this charade
of self-denial.

Time to educate ourselves
you say? Come now, isn't
it getting just a little late...

The universities are full of
us it seems... learning second
careers? Come now, when there's
no more at home... and you know
what I mean.

Isn't it just easier to bury
our desires than rekindle them
Even if it only means our own hands
going down under our own bed clothes
in the dark

The spark is worth the bit with
the two sticks, dammit.

To Feel Again

To feel again in any way
the earth pressing underneath
my shoes
packing me straight up,
reminding me of gravity,
I would be grateful.

Young and rock-fleshed once,
I pompously spoke loud
of the world's problems:
"Jimmy's crawdad's bigger'n mine"
"The sand burns my feet."
To satisfy a six-year old
a slender crayfish?
But then the importance
of my tiny desires
kept my shoes spinning.

Hunting Season

In the woods
at the home
she wears a green plaid hunting jacket
itchy over her floral print dress

and rocks on the broad white veranda
while her rattan chair
rides over the splintered, grey porch boards
like a rocking horse
carrying an angry child

She hears a gunshot.

In the woods
not far away
a flag-tailed deer is collapsing,
crumpling over its folded legs
like a lawn chair put away
for the season.

Day Dream

Where are the warm winds
that hurled soft priscillas
around my summer windows?

Once I was tall with clear
towering miles of life
moving surely like a bell
swaying through doors and
conversation; and sometimes
dreaming in grasses moist
with pansies I heard
Mother and Father
holding hands in the wind.

Shame

the day my father saw me
naked in the tub
and I rushed to cover
my tiny breasts with my
wet washcloth
and felt the quick flush
of embarrassment travel
up my soapy body
I knew he knew
he'd lost his little girl
when he said excuse me
and left

Puffed Wheat

I remember when Mother
sewed all four of us matching
green swimsuits bordered with red rickrack,
something special,
to get our picture taken in.

And the photographer came
with his magic machine
and hid under a big black cape
to see us better.
He wanted us to do something natural
'cause he said unposed pictures
always look the best.

So Mother drug out a big box of
puffed wheat and a huge slotted spoon
for us to eat it with
and while the puffed wheat rained
all around us to the floor,
we tried to put the spoon clean
in our mouths
like fearless sword swallowers.

The photographer click, clicked, clicked
under his black tent
and kept saying things like
"perfect" or "great".

The pictures came out nice
but we couldn't understand
why Mother wouldn't let us play
the "puffed wheat" game again...

She said something about
sweeping the carpet for days.

Richland (A poem to my Father)

Daddy, I remember
you striding home carrying
your big black lunchpail,
dressed in khaki,
and the space between
your front teeth when you smiled

And how you took us hiking
every Saturday
in the purple foothills
blooming with sagebrush;
how we raced each other
up the slopes
and sped down the other side.

You'd buy us orange crush or grape soda
and when we'd climbed
our little snowless Matterhorn,
we'd throw them like glass javelins
in a contest to see whose bottle
would tumble the farthest down below.

The winner got no prize:
A Father's pride is always thanks enough.

Mother

I

In zero degree weather
a little girl in a thin cotton dress
chopped wood
In zero degree weather her parents
chop chop chopped
into her pretty little heart
and would have broken
her to pieces if they could.

The love her Mama could not give
The love her Father drank away;
The love my Mother never had
left a hole as big as heaven
in her forsaken Irish heart.

II

The songs her Mama never sang
She sang to us
The love she never had
She gave to us
    without reservation.

The words she never heard
She spoke to us
The things she never learned

She taught to us
with ceaseless devotion.

There are no empty spaces within us...
O' Mother you have made us glad.

Katy

We called her Katy-Bug,
Kathleen Ellin,
the first born,
the only dark-eyed one...
  as a child her glossy black hair
fell in ringlets down her back.
She grew up fast.

She was our mother and our father
when our mother and father were gone:
Father was in Africa standing in tall grasses;
Mother was in Kansas far away from home;
Kathie was in the kitchen all day long.

Kathie was married and had two sons
Now she's divorced
and lives all alone in Hoquiam
in a house full of plants that she
tends with such care
that they thank her with rich foliage
and their leaves, like arms, reach out to say
they love her:

As we all love her.
her boys call long distance on the phone
just to say hello; they look forward each year
to their summer visits.

And now we call her Katy...
She who's had her brush with death
   and survived;
She who's run on horseback toward the setting sun
   and beyond.

She, who is just beginning to find herself.
We, who are just beginning to find her.

Mecca

I lived in San Jose all alone
with Grandma and Grandad

At night, kneeling beside
my little bed,
I said my lonesome prayers
to Jesus up above

I prayed to my Mother
to the East

I prayed to my Father
across an ocean to the South

I prayed to my brother
and my sisters to the North

My headboard was my wailing wall;
The tears I memorized in silence
all day

sang into my pillow
in broken melody.

Holden

I felt like Heidi
living in the Swiss Alps
the year I lived with my grandparents
in the tiny village of Holden,
Washington.

The Lady of the Lake
chugged past steep mountains
blooming with pine
across Lake Chelan
to the ends of the earth.

It might have been
a Norwegian fjord
so perfectly the snow
slept in the arms of the hills.

The houses were built on stilts–
so deep the snow fell
all through the long winter.

Flat on my back
pumping my arms
I made angels in the snow;
tried to catch chipmunks
(Grandpa said the trick was
to put salt on their tail).

I walked to school cautiously
along a steep trail
high above a raging river;
it hadn't been so long ago
some young boy fell and drowned
his frail body dashed to pieces,
never found.

Grandpa worked in the copper mines
where pennies are born;
Grandma crocheted gowns
for story-book dolls–
like magic, pink & blue ruffles
fell from her quick hook.

And when the Lady of the Lake
my ship of good hope
carried me safely back home like a daughter

the hours passed like waves
moving easy over water.

1224 Harrison

At 1224 Harrison
we listened to Chopin and Haydn

Now it all comes back to me
the squirrels and the chestnut trees;

the street without an end.

Summertimes were hot-white heat
Mother drove us to Lake Shawnee
Nights were electric fireflies
their pinpoint lights which mesmerized

glowed inside our mason jars.

Topeka, your Indian name
is dancing on my tongue again

At 1224 Harrison
we listened to Chopin and Haydn

on the street without an end.

Topeka Tornado

In the middle of the night
the piercing siren droned
like a crazed bee
waking the sleeping city to impending disaster.

Mother hurried us downstairs to the basement,
our little fists rubbing the last trace of
easy dreams from our eyes.

"Lady, Lady, Lady," all four of us cried
for our gun-shy pointer crouched in terror
at the screaming sound and wouldn't descend
the basement stairs.

And like running back into a burning building
to save a child,
we ran upstairs and carried our trembling pet
to safety...
"in the Southeast corner of the room," where
the radio assured would be our best chances
for survival.

We waited all night to hear the sounds
of our roof being ripped off;
of walls collapsing;
we waited for the entire house to be lifted
to the sky in one violent whoosh...

But nothing really happened.
Except for a broken bedroom window;
except for hailstones big as golfballs
on the floor.

And we were so disappointed.
For what will frighten the parent
will often thrill the child.

Bud

Cotton candy from the fair
Ferris wheel rides; a teddy bear
We each were treated separately
By this Santa-friend of our Mother, Molly.

I swear he spent his weekly salary
On each of us
On each of us
We took him into our family
But never for the money
    never for the money.

He was raised in a Wisconsin orphanage
His mother died young; his father estranged
Left the scars, never forgotten
Left a young man all but forsaken
      except for us
      except for us.

He makes a living as a carpenter
Pounding nails and such
Went to night school for a couple of years
To become an Anthropologist.

His mind is quick, his humor droll
Had me reading Pfeiffer at nine years old;
Wood is his work, humor his craft
We like him most cause he makes us laugh.
    he makes us laugh
    he makes us laugh

And that's good enough for us.

Our Lady's Shrine

One day long ago in May
we drove through Denver, Colorado
and saw the signs pointing to
Our Lady's Shrine.
Mother turned the station wagon
down the little winding road
leading slowly up a narrow
dangerous ledge
up up up to the Lady.

There she was, a large pink statue
(a little green with mold)
standing in a large shallow pool
full of holy water...
I was disappointed because
there were no lepers.

Then down the hill again
(or I should say mountain)
past hooded nuns dressed in black

Down to the highway
laughing and blessed
all the way to California.

The Great Salt Lake Desert

The station wagon bounced through Utah
while the four of us kids
played the alphabet game trying to see
who could get from A to Z first
just by looking at license plates on cars,
or billboards, or any kind of sign.

The closer we got to the Great Salt Lake
desert the more difficult the game became
but we forgot all about it
when we saw the first glimpse of the
salt desert

like a great expanse of crystallized snow
unmelted under the merciless sun.

Mother pulled over
and we all piled out
and got out little red sandpails and
toy shovels
and shovelled the salty sand til our pails
overflowed

(tasting occasionally to reassure ourselves
it was really salt).

Later that night, at the El Rancho motel,
we spent forever shaking salt out of our

sneakers and clothes
but we knew our pails were safe in the trunk
of the car

And that Grandma would be thrilled
with our gift.

Jimmy

If it hadn't been for the
John Nagy t.v. show in Spokane
with his Learn-to-Draw kits
Mother bought us one Christmas
where would you be now?

Remember shading the pumpkins
in the first lesson;
drawing the snow humped over
a country mailbox in the last?

Paper and pencil were
our favorite things:
I drew fashion models,
you drew airplanes.

But I didn't practice like you.
And when I traded art for poetry,
        A fierce determination
        A driving ambition
drove you far beyond mediocrity.

And, now, my brother
you've almost earned a
Masters degree in Architecture
from a prestigous East coast school.

As the only brother in a sea
of sisters,

you were bound to be our special one:
We're always saying, "my brother this"
or "my brother that."

And when Mother or Father speak of you
Tis with a certain, simple pride they say–
"My son."

My brother, my son:
Jimmy, your name is a song
your family sings.

Regan

She was the most beautiful of us all.
I recall her reading *War and Peace*
as she dried her long, thick golden hair
in the sun.

Her namesake is a daughter of King Lear;
She dwelt in the womb while Mother read Shakespeare.
She was the youngest child
and might have been a princess after all.

Her blue translucent eyes beguiled.
She was not wild…
Because she learned not to repeat
the mistakes of her older sisters,
I cannot say–

And if I taught her anything,
it was not to follow in my footsteps:
even the ballet shoes I once wore
dusted with rosin for dance class
serve as bedroom slippers now
without a pirouette left in them.

But that was long ago.
There are other things we have both
forgotten.

She was such a quiet girl,
yet when she laughed, her laughter
filled the house with little bells

of contagious joy.
And now with a child of her own
and one on the way,
She lives by the San Francisco Bay.

She's married to a classical musician
and the sound of string quartets
orchestrates the things she does all day.

And, not with a little regret,
I must admit I hardly knew her;
maybe I'll get down and visit in a year or two.
> After all
> She is my sister.
> And I've so much to tell,
> And so much to listen to.

Mickey and Dorothy

I can't remember who they were
or why we stayed there
It was either Los Gatos or Saratoga
I can't be sure.

I remember white rabbits
with pink eyes in pens
I saw their little hides
stretched up in the sun.

I remember the Eucalyptus
which bled its oily skin
I loved the sticky sap
A heady musk in the wind.

There were three sets of bunkbeds
pony hides on the floors
There were horsehair blankets &
every room danced with leather.

We picked apricots lazily
in the sweltering orchards
yellow jackets swarmed crazily
we heard their every word.

I can't remember who they were
or why we stayed there
It was either Los Gatos or Saratoga
I can't be sure.

Australia 1956 (for Jimmy)

Our journey to Australia by sea
Might as well have been
A watery voyage to a distant galaxy

The ship was colossus to us...
Our small feet pattered on her sunny
decks,
Our eyes patrolled the green flecks
Of wave on wave
of endless sea
Hoping to spot a whale for you,
A magical mermaid for me.

The only thing better than the trip
Upon the sea was the trip by land:
The pungent eucalyptus tree,
A kookaburra gone crazy with song
And a thousand more memories
(Twenty years old)
To you and me belong.

King Neptune

The S.S. Orcades
was crossing the equator,
All the grownups told the kids
we were passing over
King Neptune's Kingdom

And they made us get into
our swimsuits
and line up to meet His majesty
(some sailor, some game ship's officer)
with a seaweed crown
in a grass skirt
holding a makeshift triton

And one by one
we were smeared with vanilla ice cream,
had to kiss a kipper (ugh!)
held out on a pillow
by some subject of the King

Had to dive into the
ship's saltwater pool
while everyone giggled or applauded.

Boy, what grown-ups won't do
to make us think we're having
fun.

Malaspina Ranch

We once lived in a huge old house
with a name as beautiful
as the piney woods and cool clear streams
part of the five hundred acres of land

on which stood Malaspina...
Malaspina Ranch with too many rooms to count
(for the first time all four of us kids
had our own bedroom).

It came furnished and I recall with fascination
the voluminous library– with an actual card
catalog and how the books lined the parlour
from floor to ceiling and continued
in orderly fashion through other rooms of the house.

The kitchen went on forever
stretching from one end of the house to another;
there was an old wood stove plus an electric range
and outside on the veranda hung a triangular
dinner gong

once used to call in ranch hands & sheepherders
to steaming bowls of chili and baking powder biscuits
dripping with honey.

The living room was also gigantic.
An old stone fireplace dominated the room–
It was here before bedtime Mother would gather

us together by the fire and read nightly installments
from Tom Sawyer and Huckleberry Finn (I'd pretend
I was Becky Thatcher with golden ringlets– the apple
of Tom's eye).

Outside the house rose acres and acres of wheat.
After it was harvested we played hide'n seek among
the straw bales… we kept each other company;
there was no one else to play with in this isolated
countryside high in the northern California mountains.

I musn't forget Injun Joe who was sort of a caretaker
and quite mysterious. Ol' Joe kept to himself; he wore
a big black hat with a feather in it and lived in a
little log cabin down the valley from us.
We always knew Joe was home when we saw a thin curl
of smoke rise in the night air from his chimney.

Someday, I'd like to go back to Malaspina… just
long enough to say one last goodbye.

Schemes

There was the time Mother
wanted to quit her job,
move to the ocean
and rent hipboots for smelting
to Sunday campers & fishermen.

There was the time
she considered buying
her own fresh pork
to make & sell
Chinese & barbecued
from her very own kitchen.

There was the time
she came home
with 15 or 20 enormous
blue-satin, gold-braided
uniforms of some kind;
they were a real buy
and she knew we'd all
find some use for them.

There was the time
she added Cheerios
to the Jello
for a nice, crisp touch

But what a soggy, soggy surprise!

Seaview

The bugle from Fort Lawton
woke us with reveille,
put us to sleep with taps each night.
The waters of Puget Sound
lap, lap, lapped
at our doorstep like a hound.

An old wooden raft tied to a rotten beam
was our private Kon-Tiki:
we let out the rope
and rode the churning wake
of speed boats and cabin cruisers
clear to the middle of Shilshole Bay
until the Coast Guard,
fearing for our safety,
made us stop.

A deep train whistle that you hear
with your belly
would wake us from a sound sleep
and shake our little cottage
with fists of iron; fists of steam.

If we lived on the wrong side of the tracks
it never occurred to us.
Our front yard was the Sound;
the sun setting golden-red
on the snow-capped Olympics

was our private scenario
was a spectacular farewell to a seaside day.

Little Rock

In Little Rock, Arkansas, in '62
my family stayed in a big fancy motel
right downtown
why there was maids and built-in t.v.
and room service
any time of day or night

and the restaurant near the lobby
was famous for having the best
pecan pie in the South.

I had heard you got to watch out
for the "coloreds"
cause they're full of hate and
wear razor blades on their shoes.

But the only "coloreds" I ever saw
were the maids, and the waiters
in the dining room and they were
Oh so friendly and polite

always sayin' "Yes, Sir", or "No, Mam"
that I just couldn't understand
what all the fuss was about.

Kalaloch

We were excited about
going to Kalaloch
in the first place

But Jimmy couldn't get
the tent up;
the poles kept collapsing
like legs on a day-old
giraffe.

Spindly & stubborn they
finally stood
and we got to sleep in our
tent that night.

Camping

When
six o'clock
came sneaking in
we were supposed
to get up
& have fun...
playing nature lover,
pioneer,
pilgrim.

Regan at Kalaloch

She spent most all her time perched
On a cliff reading

It's a wonder she wasn't airborne

Her long, long hair billowed
Like a yellow sail behind her.

Song for my Grandparents from San Jose

Grandmother, Grandmother
I remember your home
In San Jose, California
The orange studded with cloves
   that hung from a rafter
   by the green patio.

Grandfather, Grandfather
I remember you well
Your biscuits on Sundays
That we ate to our fill
   dripping with honey
   are warm in my memory.

Grandmother, Grandmother
You had a green thumb
African violets bloomed with your care
The roses you tended sang in the sun
   their soft petals were velvet
   their perfume was fine.

Grandmother, Grandfather
You've traveled away
From the house I remember
In sunny San Jose;
   It's been a long while
   since I've seen you two
   too long a time
   'way from people I love.

But I think of you often
At noon check the mail
For maybe your letter
Instead of a bill.

Grandmother, Grandfather
It's been a long while
Too long a time
'Way from people I love.

DIVORCE

Mom & Dad don't sing anymore.
The banjo and guitar are in the closet
in the hallway with the towels
and troubles of married life.

Divorce is in the air
as sure as spring:
clotheslines don't tell
everything
but
his trousers and her skirts no longer
dry side by side in the evergreen air.

With her hair floating down
over her black cape
Mom tells fortunes and prays away mistakes.
Dad goes to night school on the installment
plan.
The sun rises in the firs here like a fan.
Far from the city, the smell of tar pitch
and wood smoke hangs in the air, acrid;
energetic.

Peace umbrellas the landscape in the form of
Mom digging weeds; Dad planting flower seeds
and dreaming of a new wife / new life.

Mom volunteers a lot and colors her hair.
She'd run away from home if she could

and start over.
I guess I wouldn't even be her daughter anymore.

Hopscotch

I remember
hopscotching down the sunburned sidewalk
down the white broken concrete
on one leg
in my patent maryjanes.

The California street was never ending;
looming walnut trees threw protective silhouettes
around me.

The oily fruit was bursting from its tight green skin
and paid me no notice, or applause
as my rusted link of chain
fell from my hand
with perfect aim.

To Mother in Kansas

...and when all the
world's asleep
you'll hear the rich
green corn
growing in your warm fields.

The Wedding

my brother got married
today in San Francisco
I didn't go to the wedding
just took a nap
and dreamed he died.

The Wish

The pink candles on grandma's birthday cake
blazed like a small forest fire
Its heat melted wax all over
the red candy rosettes.

Before grandma had time to blow them
all out
the kitchen curtains caught fire
before anyone could ask
just what her wish was

the entire house burned down
with all of us in it.

Thoughts in the First Snowfall

A flake of snow
A grain of sand
neither one
can understand
the reason why
they go their way
we know
not either
so we stray
alone,
      bewildered,
            and afraid.

The Little Frog

There was a time
when all our dreams
would fit into a jar;
a little frog,
a bit of string,
a fish shaped like a star.

The treasures we would
wish at night
were wished for
fierce and strong;
then there it was

a licorice rope
to last the whole day long.

But now the jar is empty,
our dreams won't fill it up;
it sits in a basement cupboard
gathering memories of dust.

And underneath the porch
on a still and rainy day,
you can hear a lonesome, little frog
sadly steal away.

Mallards

Iridescent green-satin heads
Strain on black & brown necks
As they lean forward into an easy swim
Across the waters of Lake Washington.

A nose dive;
White tail feathers point to the sky...
And the beaks, hard as shell
Sometimes come up with a surprise...

...A strand of duck grass;
A bit of plankton;
A crust of bread thrown by a generous
Stranger–
(Bread saved for weeks in an open bowl
atop the refrigerator).

Then they paddle off.
Their large, yellow, plastic-looking feet
Churning like the wheel of a Mississippi
Riverboat...

The Iris

Blue lips invite the dip and
taste of bees
who would go berserk
if they could not enter her.

They bumble inside,
lay waste
to her sticky yellow grape.

There is a small quiver
so brief
I fail to turn and see
the fleeting matrimony.

San Juan Day

Hear me Juan de Fuca
whales cry for their mothers
seals bleat on rock outposts

Here in the
gardens of Poseidon
where cool blue waters are
braceletted by
mountains

trouble comes.

The sun warms my face
as I ride on
the inter-island ferry

Time suspends thought.

Sawmills

Silver sawmills
sit under a bright blue sky.

Logs bob in oily water
and the only sound I hear
is the purr of saws.

The reflection of a mallard's
green helmet
erases the rainbow slick.

For one moment I sense eternity
–mill, duck, sky...
then hurry on.

Palouse

Yellow wheat fields
are plowed under
by a farmer
riding a red tractor
beneath the hastening sun.

Man & machine
purr over the rich loam
oblivious to the single
blackbird
dark in the cantilevered sky

winging its way home.

My Tree

A change has come upon my tree
which stands so straight & tall
her coat's no longer emerald green
...no leaves are left at all.

My tree has lost her color, so
becoming to the eye,
and her barren branches hover
over the hill
that once was mine.

My tree will house her friends
again
Mother Nature's children all
and keep them warm till Autumn comes
and the quiet raindrops fall.

My tree will regain her beauty, I know
when the sun shines bright
outside
and once again my tree will bloom
in her glory and her pride.

Seattle Drought

Nasturtiums trail into vines
and snake along the front walk.
The Japanese maple is profligate with
greenery and
I don't notice a single leaf falling (its
surface a hint of gold)

or the families of ants inching toward the
cracks and crevices of our house– their
teeny black suitcases in tow–

I can still pick a dozen red roses for the
dining room table and expect them to wilt
in a day or two.

Mosquitos, flies, bees worry the air
and the needlepoint covered brick which props
open the front door
is busy propping open the front door.

My cats savor the honey of sunlight
falling aslant on our warm wooden floors.
They don't notice the lawn outside has
turned the color of mead
even while

Petunias openly flirt with their petticoats
of white & pink...
When the rains come
what tropical promise waits?

Beached

Slate grey sky
Slate grey sand

I dressed against
the slate grey wind
in knitted scarf and gloves

and headed down
the hard-packed sand
(a slate-grey void)

then there it was

a slate grey whale
too big almost
to comprehend

another song silenced
in the slate grey sea

Slate grey whale
eye open in death…

Slate grey dream.

Lovelier

Lovelier than anything I could say or do
is the white swan
skirting the blue waters
when the day is through

out of reach of breadcrumbs
tossed by a few
haughty & proud she
doesn't need you

Apples

I don't feel like having one
But there's a whole box of apples
on the back porch.

Their wine-y smell
is nice on the October
air.

Last year when my mouth watered for
something besides bread and beans
I couldn't afford even one...
Now they tumble
crisply next to one another

in the big box on my back porch
and I don't feel like having even one.

The Big Tree Is Gone

Lost in an alchemy of spirit
the brown wren huddles as a small puff of life
seen in a Grant Wood painting:
orange trees, orange paths leading to a
red ochre river

reminds me that

times are bad and getting worse
neighbors up the street cut down
the biggest damned tree I'd ever seen
the sidewalk's still a snakey crack
(that tree broke my Grandma's back)

Every time I return books to the library
I pass the obscene stump.
I wonder what anesthetic could ever seal
the pain
the old tree must have felt
when the chainsaw's first angry blade
severed her trunk from base.

must have been a throb so loud
it sealed the lips of air's revenge.

The Spider

Tentacles of black nylon-thread
tripping hugely with eyes that have some sort
of "I will eat you" brain inside them.

Crawling– always coming from another dimension
under the rug, behind the refrigerator, falling
from my hair
in mornings…
not ready for brains of loathsome poison,
small (maybe to some)
but for me a giant, a germ come from the dead

An unreal reminder of… hell.

Eggs

The eggs that have fallen
from their mothers
lie in paper crates
twelve at a time.

You tell me they're
unfertilized.
Do you mean to say
their mothers slept alone?

I break them in the
pan two at a time
and pull away the
tiny white membranes

knotted like umbilical cords.
I add a little milk
and whip them up
so frothy
that I might forget
how they fell from
their mothers
before I scramble and eat
them for breakfast.

Mt. St. Helens Eruption #4 & #5

Ash clouds filled
the air
bloom upon cumulus bloom

In that hot blue summer night
streaked
with mauve and maroon

Soundlessly...
Mt. St. Helens
spilled millions of her volcanic words

Like silence follows silence
in an empty room.

Country Visit

I am new here
under the pure palace sky
so I try to name the amber fields,
            the green hills,
and the slow, silent cows
with a word of wonder toward
some secret mind
higher than yours or mine.

haiku

The sun spreads like a
fan; a fresh geisha shining
through the drawn curtains.

Lilacs

Last fall I spent hours
pruning you
clipping here and there
scooping off the dark brown
ashes of your summer work.

I watched you all winter
stark-limbed and dauntless
against the continuous
blowing rain.

I wondered, sometimes,
in a particularly driving wind
if you'd ever bloom again.

And, now, in all haste
I anticipate the first
fragrant bloom of lavender
as I see your purple clusters
of buds
         ready to burst into flower.

Ecology

When the water is all gone
the streams' dusty trails
What will we drink
but the blood of the quail.

When the oil is all gone
the gas and the coal
What will we burn
but the skin of the mole.

Whe our air is polluted
our oxygen gone
What will we breathe
but the pores of our lungs.

When the quail has died
the mole long extinct
What will we eat
but the skin of our teeth.

When our teeth all fall out
when our bones turn to rust
What will we do
when our dust turns to dust?

Uncertainty

I am hanging onto the corner of this desk
afraid to fall into the sea of carpet
beneath me.

My eyes are weak compasses
seeing only north , and then
falteringly.

I have a lifejacket shaped like this
cigarette
and I smoke and tug till I know the water's calm.

Perhaps, if I play my cards right,
I'll drift to my bedroom
and sleep or drown

There is nothing certain
about a ship going down.

Depression for Breakfast

Linty leotards stretched on
in the dizzy hour of day
I laboriously rake the
half-clean comb
through bed-tangled hair
and unfold the morning paper
to movie ads.
Nothing new.
I move to
the chipped cupboard
and accidently spill
oatmeal on
the grimy burner.
It will smell horrible now
for days.
I don't feel
like eating, anyway.
I finally reach the bathroom
and not being meticulous,
hurriedly use my toothbrush.
Avoiding the clean mirror,
I hurry
to get my coat.
In my arm goes– conscious
of the movement.
I'm ready.
I walk towards the no-longer
Little red schoolhouse.
So regimented. Everyone

sitting in his (or her)
little seat and pretending to read
his (or her) textbook.
I feel vomity.
I won't visit the nurse
who doesn't give a damn anyway.
I leave
the building not caring
about trivial consequences.
I go home.
I turn on the television.

The Crazy Boy

Hands like bony spiders
reach and toy
roughly with other people's wasted
cigarettes. Then fly wildly
to make sure his hair is here.
A comb, a spider dance...
He's beautiful now.

Insanity

Sway, sway, sway
Slowly first– moving into a motion
equal to Viking rowers.
Back and forth. Back and forth.
Motion faster than the diamond-capped
waves, pushing through impassable air,
through discordant symphonies,
Through, through... faster, faster
Faster, faster
Faster than the knife,
the pill,
the broken-bridge,
the jet-age death.
Spin, spin the
Merry-go-round of insanity...
Faster
   faster
      faster
         faster

I Think I'd Like To Go To The Hospital

I think I'd like to go to the hospital, dear

and get away from it all
have the doctors comfort me & sit around the halls
                        just smoke a little
                        & rap a lot
with anyone who's a little crazier than me– maybe

But then on second thought those halls get awful
stark
& the beds are hard and that one navy blanket won't
keep me warm

I'd just cry your name into my pillow
& want you there–
I know I just couldn't wait to come home to you

I know I just couldn't wait to come home to you
to be my daddy and my brother and the boy up the block
I played kick the can with
to be my lover & that flirtatious stranger
to be my god to be my little boy to be my husband
to be the thousand people I need to rock me to sleep
tonight.

manic-DEPRESSION

sometimes I feel so worthless
I feel like someone is step-
ping on me.

To die is to know no more anticipation
of death;
like eating popcorn in an empty theatre...
the gargantuan curtains are closed.

No more coming attractions;
Just adjustable seats.

As a kid I wondered what the Loges were...Now
I know. They're roped off...

Even here in the empty theatre I don't trespass.
I walk all the way down to the first three rows;
walk halfway in row number two and await my own death
as the rustling purple curtain parts.

Off to the left is a faint green EXIT
if I change my mind.

MANIC-depression

The roller coaster is as high
as it will go...

We scream our throats raw
as the rickety tracks detour out over the ocean
and jerk back again.

The safety bar barely holds us in.

I want to do it all again
without restriction.

Rush Hour Traffic

The car is electric death
breathing, burning tin & flesh

Chrome of brains and sadist-built.

rolling around and pushing
through the town
of air and wheels and nightmare screeching.

Bodies weak and mortal

H A T I N G

Wondering if I will ever get out of this cage alive.

The Pillow Maker

And I took this wild fawn, this
tender kicking fawn into the
rooms with a thousand doors
that never open.
And she longed to run away
into the green of Ireland and
spend her waking years upon
the banks of Shannon.

And she cried for love she ran to find
and she cried for love she ran to lose
and she still pads softly
among the Chinese-puzzle rooms.

And she cries– this wild fawn–
for the green of Ireland
and she cries for her pure pastoral
homeland...

And with her hands
she fashions softness gently
into pillows.

Coming of Age

Every woman likes to think
she is desirable...
water on rock
slips easily into
forgetfulness

She studies the size of
her breasts
in her telling mirror
at night–
silicone
haunts her dreams
on a white horse–

Water tugs her off the bridge
in her gown of skin;
hell is waking up on impact
with nowhere to go
but back to sleep.

Chicken Little, Chicken Little

Chicken Little
Chicken Little.
The sky is falling.
You know, you felt the first blunt
particle as it spun against your tiny
head. And how brave you were in your
own small way, toting a prophet's necessity
of warning upon your furry shoulders.
But Chicken Little, where do you hide?
Are you alive
or half-alive
or dead
or half-dead?

It began yesterday afternoon
when the sky darkened. And slept surrealistically
against my open window.
This morning; no wind. And then the clock stopped
its elementary melodies.
And then the crowd of marionettes
calmly exploded.
Puff. Their strings left dangling
as the sky swallowed them up;
smiles, briefcases– all.

Chicken Little Chicken Little.
the sky is falling,
And He has locked
the asylum door.

Ward G

The knobs of fate
break in my hands
The ominous door ajar

With gentle Bertha hailing
me, her arms
hold up a chair.

While Bertha soothed
her childlike heart,
the chair across the room
flew as I ducked
into Mary's lap and
said a prayer for two.

The doors of light
opened quick... then
shut my Mary into locks
and gentle Bertha
knelt by me...
    "My little saint",
    she laughed.

I Am Christmas

I paste coloured pictures on collages
and feel like I am Christmas
hanging brilliant globes upon
my tree.
And though the voices are not caroling
and the gingerbread lies sleeping
I am Christmas
and see myself reflected in my tree.
And one for love and one for woe
and one for Spring who melts my snow.
I'll be
Christmas without the virgin ground
And I'll be
Christmas without the breath of
Santa on my stairs–
Without anyone, without anyone
I will be Christmas.
Sometime… try and be your own
Christmas.
See love sit with her head
in her hands as she stands
delicately in vases.
Feel love in music and let
your body be the harp of angels.
Touch love laced through ivory elephants
touch this dormant love
and if you can stand it–
Even close your door– lock it–
Be your own Christmas.

Paste your last picture– and
do not scream for companionship.

I Am Lost Too, Plato

O' to lie down in my own craziness,
to open my arms to conceivable
demons and kiss them behind the
cellar door of sensuous sorrow.

Sorrow climbs my steady spine,
reaches a place we call heart
and
I accept my demons because
all the men I ever knew
have retired to their locker rooms,
are feeling beautiful with their
pictures of anonymous nudes
and lie down in their own dreams.

And I plead: kiss me spirit friend
kiss me into night– and
never show your face
against the kitchen light;
for my lost love waits
through his golden maze
and I hope not
your kiss be death
before my days are through.

It is not fair. Great men
patent my ideas before
I am born.
And then cannot I say,

Cannot I bend and say:
I am lost, I am
lost too, Plato?

For e.e. cummings

(someday;
What fool
Gropes
To rise above
Baseness
And
Pettiness,
To become ethereal
To acquire thoughts
From posthumous minds;
Only to lie
Dead).

Brilliance Lie Down on a Friday Afternoon

Please sun. Touch me gentler.
Rock the leaves into a
gray iridescence.

Grass. Pull in your long–
Stemmed fingers of Spring
Before your greeness
Blinds me.

Sky. Choose a different
Cathedral to be proud in;
Dash your blue against
A stronger soul.

Sea. Taste your own salt.
Lie down in your own wake;
And invite me on a
Gentler day…
                And this poet walked away.

The Hour Just Before Dawn

The silent hedges appear as
Two shadowed sheep–
Shorn to necessity in their
Lane upon the concrete.

The darkness echoes to each
Other and doors
Tremble each unfamiliar
Voice.

Fear and my hand do not draw
The curtain to greet this hour
This hour of
No greeting.

Restless every morning.
This hour a confused child
Asking the way home.

Hair

Men don't know hair.
It passes from them
like silk from a cob

In their middle years... soon
the countable strands
to comb.

Women know hair.
It grows long in the evening
by an open fire.

In middle age
down come the braids and combs
of years

the result of steadfast patience
and boar bristle brushes.

I thought I knew hair.
I grew yards of it.
I was promised love in excess
each chestnut inch.

Passersby exclaimed:
"a horse's mane!"
Their oohs and ahs
meant riches, love and all.

The scissors rust in my hand.

Me & Howard Hughes

I'd pay for your kids' teeth
if only you'd be my friend.

It's this desert
that's so hard to take.
My canvas canteen clatters
on the highway.

My checkbook
is as good as worthless
with no water nearby.

For a drink of water
I'd give you
a million dollars.
Honest.

These lizards are bold
and I'm afraid...

Not even a cactus stands
nearby
to tide me over.

I'd eat it like watermelon
just for the juice
and ignore the thorns.

A flower would be nice, too.
In fact I'd give it to you.

Prisoner

The rope was always there,
draped through the bars of my
stone cell.

The Visit

Don't look through light communally –
for the light of common day
will never be common.
Common
are your fears
your body lost in years
the perpetual tears
which stain no one's cares but your own.

Man apart in body
must seek his own mind
travel down his own
corridors of consciousness
until he finds
the truth.

And others of his kind
will feign at being blind
will weep against their brother
will deny for a million Sundays
Their loneliness.

He liked me and so I loved him

"He liked me and so I loved him." Tennessee Williams, *Suddenly Last Summer*

What a way he entered my aura of friendliness,
The way we smiled– our heads bowed
In beautiful acknowledgement; and now
I try to see him clearly
But he moves unfocused like an
over-used t.v. rerun.

I see, now, only his strong shadow
Which slowly fades like Seattle when
The fog sleeps heavy for days
Upon the stone-gray buildings.
His kisses, like all my memories
have faded

I try, I cry to shine his image
Stonger. but I smile and say
Bravely:
> Chin up. He has gone. I will
> Leave all my sparrows to fly
> to Capistrano in splendor.

Cabin Fever

These walls are suffocating me.
They are hands of ether-filled rags
coming closer, closer.

I've counted the leaves on the wallpaper
so many times
that its mauve forest is choking me.

I'm a flower gone to seed.
I sit paralyzed on the couch
and count imaginary weeds
growing out of the carpet.

There are two windows and a door.
but my key won't fit the latch;
the windows are high...
and my ladders are all broken.

The Orphanage

The air is heavy with the
odor of warm blood
as a feather settles
in the stainless steel kitchen.

Ma Brown stations herself
over a kettle the size of a corn
bin and arranges homemade maple
bars sweet as sin.

Once a month twenty orphans
eat their fill, say a thankless
grace
and wish for home.

Swingsets freeze on the winter lawn
as the curtains close.

Doctor K

My seeking met a man in the gentle
grayness of your smile.
O', private one-room love,
I've come to you with needs no
God can solve.

Your hand upon my hair reveals small faiths

I cannot call you now except in sighs;
(amidst shuttered telephones I lie)
   apologizing for the
   God I've made of you
I say good night to dolls this lonely hour.

I Remember Listening

I remember listening to him,
crouching motherly,
near enough to touch him
yet far enough to sense
our growing apart.

My face, over-anxious to listen,
was tight with ridiculousness
and my mouth– soft with love–
froze within the radius of his words.

Tonight, alone and reading love stories–
I feel my body close,
to think tomorrow he might return
only to grow completely away.

Definitions

I'm an empty cup in a china case
decorative but seldom used;
the tremor in a voice can leave
me broken for days:
      speak softly in my house of glass.

I'm a soufflé in the oven
airy and full of holes;
my peaks and valleys
collapse at the slightest noise:
      walk softly in my house of air.

I'm a Raggedy Ann doll
whose sawdust has all run out;
only the little heart that says
i love you remains:
      touch me softly in my paper house.

Oranges

I fed you oranges
one week past
and touched your face
not seeing me

Darkness reeked
of strangeness then
and words, unthought,
filled the void.

Puppets
needn't feed each other.
They laugh
at
ripe oranges.

The Coffeehouse

You talk, your back to me like some
strange wall,
asking the proprietor for new jokes
and a cup of hot cider.
Not seeing me you see me more
than the fidgety youth across
my table looking in my eyes.
Folded I am in large woolly
shirt, but naked.
"I'm sorry," she said (for another
abrupt night)
"I'm sorry for the
game you could not play."

"Smiles of a Summer Night" the
words float from orchestras
above the ceiling– bellowing down
boring into my sensitive ears.
Not raising my eyes
shadows of men jerk by– seemingly
you. But no, time saves you
(unlike the others) as you sit
five minutes more, profile only,
nailed to the wobbly bench.

You laugh your own laugh still
you laugh,
oblivious of sweat-eyed poets
lasting on empty stomachs.

For a moment you look weak
a smiling lamb pushed from the brunt of Our Lord's staff
Being only a man
and laughing as only a man must.

Seahorse

Ten lunar months will pass
I will be round as the
moon;
My little ivory seahorse
will grow out of her sea.

She will dream in a bed
smaller than me
with a name on her wrist
which stands for lovely.

The Walk

joy
in the calm wilderness
of longing,
three girls with child
rise against the
silent shore.

                              then sit on driftwood
                              desiring only the
                              sun's reflection upon
                              their faces…
                              this,

and nothing more.

Boyfriend

You...
far away,
hidden by telephone poles and my
nightmare love fantasies,
talk to me of sensitive flowers
whistling in the wind thru the bones of my
hurricane lovers.

Rock

me gently thru the shadow of past misfortunes
and wait for me til
Josie leaves my womb...
Maybe I'll be a woman then
in my naked emptiness...

All alone I will come to see you.

Repose

Her heart secure in the
woman part of me
beats tiny under
my open hand.

The smile I've hidden
all day, I smile
And I name her
once again.

All Words the Leaves Are

All words the leaves are:
abundant flickering birds of pale green,
texturing the evening with
softest symmetry.

This is the landscape I'm allowed
to share with no one.
I would call my dearest friend and say
I love you because the trees are green
and because I know there is a God;

But he is busy with his own life and
somewhere
deep inside me an anonymous baby stirs.

End of the World

The world ended today.
The prophet said so.

But here I sit...
Earth, sky, pounding baby of life knocking
my transversed flesh–
Within these walls we lie, two breathing survivors
of the holocaust.
(At the sea's shore we sit amongst half-naked
bean-pole boys wading the tides
for a gift of anything new and strange.)

I would not have been alone in death.
Early this morning I waited for the beautiful
oblivion.
Singly, I could not pull the shade on two heart beats.

But today mortality lies in the wind's conscience.
And the wind does nothing...
but send the wet splashes of tide gently to my feet.

Acceptance

Slowly I leave this growing body
and dream continuously
of all the things I might do
on bountiful barren tomorrows.

She moves...

I return.
Awaiting a catalogue dress,
I return.
To what a pretty rosy woman I will be
with my long hair
climbing over my rounding breast.

The Beautiful Movement

Perpetual years grow
backwards over
sodden earth and
damp trees.

The pregnant girl desires
him who is not there;
desires what is real,
as society's child
grows unnamed in her
swollen virginal nakedness.

Her ringless hand lies
alone on the beautiful
movement.

Time: Parts 1 & 2

She hurries thru here with
a clock in her face
which tick-tocks a
punctuated vigilance.

As the hands press
crazily past her eyes
She tries to organize
our lives.

She sits over there
with a clock in her face
which shows us the
time of her waiting.

No little Swiss man
with his delicate hands
could repair
her slow clock-broken
sorrow.

Visions of Never

White wine flows over the green valleys
and I have seen the hair that grows under
the womb of the earth... so open, so waiting
For the seed of natural order...
as somewhere a baby is being born who has no
earthly father

only a sad young mother who had to finish school in
a convent.
Just because she has seen the vision of never;
Still she has to wait for the moon to come round
nine times... nine nine nine and the Trinity is
diminished as the seas argue over fishing rights.

See the soil is being sucked of oil; less lubricant for
His grasses remains. Alas, the untied shoes
of Einstein lie golden in a cluttered museum somewhere
where only spiders know why they build cities of gloss;
Gossamer directions wiped out by the lame janitor's broom–

in the evening he is all alone as he wipes out the web.

Outside, Drying my Hair

I write the same poem
a thousand times:
what is mine is not mine.

We rock whisperingly together
inside alabaster
tenderness.

Here, above the sea,
sheltered in a landscaped
rose patch,
I love the good growth

and know that tomorrow
a red sun
will proclaim one closer day.

Pulling Weeds

The weeds in my garden grow tall.
I should have known
you'd return again to dance into my wailing arms.

    The baby's gone.
    It had no name;
    just two arms and a face
    that did not look like you.

What did you expect
from such rough sex?
Another messiah
in swaddling clothes.

And now you stand
so tall in all your nerve
to claim the bastard
with both our eyes.

But I'm all alone here
with my empty work;
only the umbilical tug of the dandelion
keeps my grief alive.

The Children I Never Had

The Children I never had
would have been grown by now...
some gone to cities far away
others across town
in condos or apartments with
rooms of many kinds
full of books, babies, Nintendo

they would know the fine art of
verbal self-defense, of dressing for
success–
ties bright birds of their own choosing–

would jog
raise environmental Cain,
debate the spotted owl and old
growth trees,
dam rivers, and damn politics
take up joysticks instead of guitars.

The girls
would tolerate me
my poetry and
felicitation of love in all its stages,
would call at least once a week
to tell of children fed,
married hurts in the flame of
togetherness,
the price of gas,

the long commute,
breakfast food.

The children I never had
would forget my birthday
remember Mother's Day
with a limp card and crisp bouquet

The children I never had
die in the egg
or the egg dies

I press dried flowers into scrapbooks
they never gave me.

Pinocchio

Oh Geppetto
That we weep and kneel
at this wooden doll
propped in our spare clean house
under a blaze of white stars
and blue sky

Our eyes grow dim in the
candle light
after years of wanting
what we cannot have

Song for Robert

My love is not a secrecy
My mouth is stung
by honey bees

My love is not a silent song
I sing your poems
into songs

My love is not a guarded thing
I wear your arms around
my dreams

My love is not a secrecy
Your words become
my legacy

And when you read this secret song
to wear on winter's mountainsong,
You'll know our secret secrecy
will rise when thyme & clover meet

When secret words become the song
all may sing at quiet morn.

I Am Joy Beside You

You are my child.
I climb through your sweet body and know that the
spacious skies of your gentleness are eternally
lovely and warm for me.

You are my friend
I watch your eyes touch my breasts with whispers
for the small and white roundness I give to you.

You are my lover.
I want to be snow for you.
Saved for you, my body remembers only you.
The quiet pleasure, the sweet pain breaking over me.

You are my earth-bound traveller, the hope of tomorrow,
the rain shimmering on our lake...
I love you.

You are my special "I-want-to-kiss-you" man.
You are my future.
I am joy beside you.

The Radio & Roses

I

I heard you come in when I was with him.
I brought you coffee stirred with cream;
I was wearing clean hair and a dissolute
sadness

I wanted to write you a help-note and put
it in a milk bottle, and hand it to you
before you left

I was wearing my glasses and typing so fast
that "he" told me to stop, and I did and I
listened to you talk about "her"

II

The next day you brought roses and smiled
at my bandages; you thanked me for lending
you music to dream to. I thought "he" had sent
you, and I prayed that he didn't.
       You helped me walk down the halls of
the hospital
       You were so shy, I wanted to die

Instead, I believed that you came on your own.
You came on your own, carrying roses and poems.
You came on your own, carrying roses and poems.

Life With Him

Life with him
is towels draped over cardboard boxes,
plastic taped over broken windows,
and peeling linoleum

But I learned at thirty
that possessions mean nothing...
I'd live in the woods; eat berries
if he could guarantee eternal spring

and there is nothing
money can buy except maybe a can of white paint
for the front porch
where I sit in the dappled sunlight

wishing nothing more
than for him to come home.
we are two lovers
running towards each other
across an open field of wildflowers

Robert and One Cat Sleeping

Your body seems
heavy as a houseful of concrete,
you sleep.

A kitten keeping
you company
is safe from all slumping beasts.

There you are, the two of you
dream upon dream

And the dream is so deep & clear
that if I were to wake you now
balanced, perhaps,
over a raging cliff

I am sure you would fall
through real air
and never wake up

I Pull Apart my Napkin at Dinner

I pull apart my napkin at dinner
over the plexiglass table
of another restaurant,
and am all nerves before you.

The monthly chant begins:
a litany of moodiness
and you listen
just like you never heard before
my self-derision.

But I'd rather be a mistress
than a wife.
I could say I was "tied up" for
seven days
and you'd never have to see
my darker side...

Just handsome lingerie
and polished hair,
an educated lady without a care,
no stale mascara or pallid prayers;
no hesitant desire to be forgiven
for another twenty-eight days.

Married

It's true.
You've let me sleep alone
again.

You make love
to late night t.v.
in your easy chair

& honey, it must be real good,
you fall asleep
right after.

The Night You Came Home Late

and when the kitchen sits alone
nor full of you a tinkering...

and ne'r a footstep shall be
heard– of yours
in the living room.

I check the basement, concrete
floors,
but just see magazines
and clothes.

no you there either,
I feel lost...
I search the house
for notes you've left.

The bed is empty
rumpled still–
from our two breathings
nighttime through.

this house is empty lord
without
my man a livin' in.

Separation

When I'm away from you–
gone
When you're away from me–
alone
the world is a stranger
too soon–
this city a planet;
grey sand
(with rooms of moss which
muffle this land)
Your echo from these walls
calls me back home
home to your arms, your heart
& our love.

These Hands

These hands these lovely hands
  that once
  in slippered warmness were
gloved against all winter could create
  have now been bared to labor long and damp
over the soapy dishes and the frying pan.

They serve me well.
The lines etched in curving pattern
on my palm bring back clear memory of all the
  years have done.

This ring this pretty little ring
  upon my wedding hand
is the everlasting circle
round our love
which stands untarnished and singular
and grand.

These hands my lovely hands
someday each one will wear
amethyst and sand.

Your Dream

Barefoot girls in calico dresses
walk through your dreams.

It is always summer
it is 90 degrees.

They are beautiful and chew grass stalks.
I know that you kiss them.

When you wake, your mouth
is stained lawn-green

Fortieth Birthday

He has integrity
He is almost forty
& painfully aware
   that he has almost failed

whether he says / or not that he cares
that he never got that red t–bird in his freedom days

(the days of laughing stoned to the mouth
 midnight to San Francisco-midnight smoke-ins
and free lunch)

He does.

To succeed, he wears the wall he built;
the wall he built with stones, and implacable pieces of his heart

He is not a funny man;
even though he makes everyone he meets, laugh…
I have seen the dark sensitive child contemplating stars.

He is too sensitive to bleed
and if he does, the cut finger heals alone;
even his wife does not blow on the ragged tear.

He worships cats.
the sleeve alone would not be cut if the mandarin robe
were occupied.

He believes he is alone; that his wife is a painless burden
and that she loves him; but that the
love is not quite enough.

In the confessional of the mirror
the razor pauses...
then hurries on.

He has candles to blow out.

fancy words

Mute– my pen scratches across the page
waiting for the ink to speak of its own accord.

Silent– my pen moves between the lines–
quickly before the hand might still the eye
that tries to lengthen

quietness
into words to form a poem
to give you.

Saying in much more fancy words than this...
I love you.

Earth, Water, Fire, Air

Your love is to me as eternal as the sea.
No red tide, nor blue death
Can diminish what was meant to be.

Your love is to me as eternal
As the dust,
No archeological dig, nor sandstorm
Can diminish what was meant to be.

Your love is to me as eternal
As the air.
No smoky city, nor foretold doomed cities,
Can diminish what was meant to be.

Your love is to me as eternal as Earth,
Water, Fire and Air;
I shall love you now– and...
For light years more.

No time can bind us, no law too taught:
Know our life together is happiness enough.

"You"

It has been years since I wrote a poem for you
yet I prattle on about how good I am
just unsung.
I speak more intimately to my reflection in the mirror
than to you
waiting on your end of the couch for a song or two.

Oh God how the years fly by
the stained glass hung in our front window changes
hue and I mark time only by the depth of red
in the red glass at eight and two; not you.

This morning for the first time
I noticed the muscles in your upper arms and remembered
you are working for our living
on your poor back trapped in the dark
underbelly of rotting houses– the huge spiders
scurrying over you.

The cocker spaniel in your brown eyes asks for a kiss
goodbye if only I would stop straightening long enough
to look at you. Darling, when you left today
I knew I hardly knew you. I watched you maneuver out
the driveway & I held back from tapping on the glass

something inside told me to let you go this time in
your brave way
you've saved my life I'm grateful I love you.

The Fog

The fog surrounds me like a lover
  in a bed of spent desire
    like the bed of love we tire
      when the moon is high and wide.

O' the moon is high and wide
  and rides around the tide
    like two lovers lost forever...
      yet a second has elapsed.

Let this fog come closer, closer
  and hold me as you chose to
    in a world of more forevers
      than the moon above the shore.

The Flaming Carousel

The men on the flaming carousel hide their faces
when they whirl past me, as I act grown-up on the
Carnival lawn. They are laughing, but
they dare not look into my eyes.
They are laughing because I will never let them off
the carousel.
What could they do but laugh?

The first one, astride the dapple-grey, knows why.
He knows he refused to grasp my poor hand on that
summer afternoon. He knows he tossed my verses
upon the sand.
And look at me watch them ride out their lives,
being as productive as they will ever be again.
Yes, I am a wise Midas gathering the golden rings
they toss.

The second one, leaning into his cherry-stallion,
laughs louder than the others and never misses the
clown's mouth with his polished rings. He
remembers, too, but does not care.
He has always liked the carousel.

There are many more of the lost and captured
riding the flaming circle of my vengeance.
Those who never came back– those who spoke, sang, and
ran
hilariously into the drunken town.
They all hide their faces from me now.
As I act grown-up on the carnival lawn.

Take Away

Take away her long soft hair
Take away her features fair
Take away her smiles & flowers
Take away the nighttime hours
Take away her smooth white skin
Take away her dimpled chin
Take away her body
Take away her body
  What have you now?
  "Nothing anymore"
  Now you have her heart
  Naked, naked heart.
  Love her heart sweet boy.
  Prove your love sweet boy.
    "Go to hell dear girl
    Now I have no girl."

Three Days After

You, not I, drew the dark upon us
And
Lifted my mouth to your mouth
Tipping me doll-like
Against you.
The room was swollen with
Our being there
(Twining shadow with kisses)
And you, not I,
Forgot three days after.

Beauty

What is beauty?
Beauty is the gentle touch
   of a mother's loving hand
Beauty is kindness…
   or to understand
one another in times of need.

What is beauty?
Beauty is satisfaction on this
   earth so carefully woven
Beauty is grace
   tenderly in motion
Beauty is honesty
Important as life itself

What is beauty?
Beauty is life… withholding
   many things,
It is the sweetness of springtime
the break of dawn, or
the sound of laughter joyously ringing;

What is beauty?
Beauty is love.

Museum

At one time
I wanted someone to
walk through my house,
a museum of myself,
and see the doilies and afghans
all hand-made
and comment on my industrious,
fine hands,
fingers swift as hummingbird wings,
fingers with Ph.D's

Someone would pick up my discarded
notebooks,
rave over the small graffiti
I might have written on the
plywood boardwalk
(braceleting another urban monolith).

But…
here is the hot furry smell
of t.v. (like tinfoil in your teeth)
encasing the room in a brittle light

When we turn it off…
Our wood stove is a huge lump of coal
in the blackness.
You and I are lit by little slices
of topaz warmth;

we stumble toward goodnight.

Wild Spiders

("We are like a lot of wild spiders crying together" Robert Lowell)

It is hard to be more sincere than we;
Now crouched under winter
And the rain.
Our small rooms attempt a crayon brightness
With one dollar prints
And Chopin's Polonaise.

Again...
Upon the bristly davenport I try
To tell you that I love you
But we are like a lot of wild spiders
Crying together–
Destructive in our helplessness.

Do Not Ask

Passionless and stiff I lean beside you
hoping you won't try to hold my hand
or breathe too quietly upon my face.
I've been hurt– my eyes say–
when you ask– your eyes say–
Lean upon my morbid body
press my heart apart with the
tips of your slender feet
and do not ask me if I love you.

Private Warmth

Climbing out of the pyramids of people;
some drunk, some sad, some sane;
I look beyond the
bridge of my horizons
beyond the kissing people...
to a private warmth– to
the heavy body and light mouth
of my unforgotten lover.

Let Us Run Away Together

Let us run away together
and live– not in an attic room
where illicit lovers always live–
But in that big white house
on Maple Street.
And we'll buy silver and a
vacuum cleaner with all the
atttachments and
we'll do our shopping every
Saturday at the bargain mart.

And we'll have kids and
carry them to the zoo
and buy them peanuts for
the elephants.
And when the time comes for
us to make love, we'll
wrap the children
and set them in the snow.

Another Dream

You love the stranger most within me
the perfect woman walking through your dreams
wearing a white gown only and carrying
lit candles through rooms awash with midnight

A woman without imagination– guileless–
padding through the chambers of your heart.

First Love

Though father said "I forbid it"
Still we hid in the tall wheat
and smoked our first cigarette.

And though mother said "I forbid it"
Still we lay together in the summer heat
and did it.

The south pasture turns our
ancient cigarette butts over
with her arms of soil

Your semen is a white sea
beneath the green lawn
beautiful
and
still.

Passion's Pragmatism

She touched his ivory brow and
knelt close, pressing delicately against
his breathing body.
Dark night.
He confessed world fears
and laughed of childhood vacant lots
and forgotten bee graves.
    Three days passed...
He stood erectly at her door,
(would not remember nonsensical play
words or the warm darkness of
their last visit)
Brusquely returned the book, spoke
long enough to tell her "how well
things were going,"
and left.

Dress-Up

She threw on blonde wigs
held her stomach in with a will so strong
she could have
lifted the house on her shoulders–

shaved in secret places
in card shapes... the heart was his
favorite with its bristly arrow–

tucked her butt in
applied 3 coats of the blackest mascara
Fred Meyer sold

wore the heels she couldn't walk in
without
balancing on his arm

wished she might have attracted the wrong
sort of
men

sailors from the 50's maybe
or cowboys from the wild west all cowhide & sweat...

i do this
 just to keep you

i do this just to celebrate the
night of Saturday

Just to.

Forgive Me Friend

Forgive me friend, if I may call
you friend,
for drinking your brandied wine
and laughing while your arms
spun me warm along the
sanded floor.
Forgive me friend for wanting
to touch
your eyes and kiss a smile upon
your sleeping beauty face.
Forgive me friend for
trying to bottle time,
for drawing you in.
But most of all
forgive me our lying
back to back.

No, Not Madly

Not madly, no not madly
Do we silently fall into each other.
Nor wildly, no not wildly
Do we taste the fresh sown mouths
We bend together.

Softly and gliding over the
Shadows of you, I climb into
Caverns, the strong silent caverns of you.
Warm you say, and warm I know and warm

The place we breathe and smile.
And smile my love smile.
And our eyes are not ashamed
And my face expects the tilt of yours,
The downward glance;
The mountainous loveliness.

Ballad

If I could see through
sadder eyes
the earth so pale at noon

Then maybe I would
miss the one
I used to call my own

The woman so blessed
with gentleness
would make even
the heather whisper

and any young man
to see her stroll the land
would sell his soul
just to kiss her.

Wanting You

Wanting you and loving you
with the breath of the wind
which blows through my blouse
and twinkles the ripe leave shadows
at my feet,
knowing you won't come back
for days or months
I pour my broad peasant smile
upon the pancake faces of everyone.

Shortbread

The creaming of the butter,
The adding of the salt,
The stirring of the sugar,

The long, slow kneading
    of the flour,
While the muscles in
Your upper arms bulge like apples.

You are a pink and white woman.
The flour serves you well:
It is white powder for your soft face;
It is your hands, your bent fists
moving over such simple ingredients

To make the sweetest confection
On earth.

The Whore

You come to her for tenderness
She wears black lace at dusk
You have no other place to go
She will not call it lust

Her room is softly patterned
Van Gogh hangs on her walls
The books she's saved from college
Are stacked in her front hall

Her eyes wear wisdom in their youth
Her legs are fine and strong
You know she'll never answer
When you ask why she belongs

To this ancient profession

Instead, being a good & lovely whore
She takes you to paradise
On waves of gentleness

And for so much loveliness
She doesn't charge you fare.

Two Rondelets

I will not go
Regardless of the season or the hour
I will not go
Until I've seen the last sweet flake of snow
Until earth no longer pushes up each flower
Until I've seen the glory, felt the power
I will not go.

###

If you must love me love me slow
The world spins fast enough
If you must love me love me slow
Haste makes waste the saying goes
Touch me gently, never rough
The candle's out with just a puff
If you must love me love me slow.

Sad Haiku

Love cannot be lone
my pain and blossoming joy
must have touched you.

Imperial Dream

My love walks nightly in an imperial dream,
fasting on persimmons
and like fruits of the mind.
He sits 'neath his wild palm
and we try to out love each other.
We both sit 'neath the wild
and we try to out love each other.

My love sings nightly in an imperial dream,
fasting on oranges
and like fruits of the mind.
He sings under mosaic canopies
and we try to out sing each other.
We both sing 'neath the wild
and we try to out sing each other.

My love aches softly in an imperial dream,
fasting on me,
and like fruits of the mind.
He cries on the threshold of
our conjugal bed
And we try to understand each other.
We both weep 'neath the wild
 and we try to understand each other.

Change of Season

My God. The sun erupted every morning
for three years; The leaves
changed six times– never tiring
of their perpetual task.
I watched the outdoor sun
spill over my young body
and never saw my own seasonal growth.

Your eyes spoke songs and
our minds fell into each other.
Three years, three long years
ago we met.
I spoke my words– but
really cared more about
the falling sun than your
careful replies. I could
not bind my own swift legs
and I longed to run
past you... into some new grove of brilliant season.
I ran– my blue eyes veiled–
and I never turned around
when you said you loved me.
Now I am your young spotted fawn
(or maybe I should say my color's fading?)
I laugh at my settling sportiveness;
at my poor blind eyes–
and I look at you
and say:
Take my hand.

Larry

walking out softly toward the
rain,
I
warm wonderfully at the tiny scarlet circus of my brain
and I laugh fluttering
for the names I've named
my love
       for you;
       silent in the sky.

for a while,
the shape of this tree (rain–y velvet blue),
I lean against
fits me more perfectly
than the color of your smile

I wonder where you are.

Bouquets

I

I'd bring you a freshet
of violets and green clover
prettier than any
greeting card with a stream
and a deer, upriver
from yellow buttercup and blue
spruce.

I'd be telling you in my awkward
but
direct way
that I love you.

You'll wash a little jelly jar
–the four ounce size–
fill it with these flowers,
bedazzled
by emerald shapes and purple
bloom.

II

The backyard goes ungardened
all the books are read
we weed our lives of need
like tulips turning red.

Mountain Climbing

small enough to
make a giant of my hand
light enough to mail
with a few postage stamps

these kittens
scale the long smooth face
of my leg, ankle to calf

& pitch camp on the treacherous
plateau of my knee

the blue half-moons of my eyes
pulse over them

they try to climb the tangled
ropes of my hair
chestnut tendrils damp & fair

their tiny breath
is white
in this cold steep air.

Kitten on the Keys

My kitten typed me a poem
today
j k l m lu
I looked in her eyes
and she replied
that spells
I love you.

Two Cats

Porcelain cat upon a windowsill
forever washing–
a captive of the potter's wheel.

My warm-maned cat with the marmalade purr
washes beside this fragile statue.
All afternoon porcelain and fur
in unison groom.

Marmalade & porcelain keep their eye upon:
the slightest leaf-stirred tree,
a robin plump with worm,
the sun suffuse & warm.

Animal and statue– warm glass, cool fur,
My windowsill is busy
with their being there.

Nine Lives

Of your many promised lifetimes
I hope this isn't your last
For I've just one, my little one,
and sand slips through the hourglass.

To me, this is your last & first
I'll teach you all I know
of how to clean & how to wash
for I have read Paul Gallico.

Oh how absurd I will look
pretending to be a cat;
down on all fours on the kitchen floor
with my leg sticking over my neck.

I'll teach you to guard your tail
from people and their shoes;
how to carry it high, my little one,
so they won't step on you.

There are so many lessons here
I cannot teach you every one;
Sharpen your tooth and nail
and always be ready to run

from: headlights
      the furious crowd
      the empty plate
      young boys with nothing to do

the pouring rain and
the scalding sun.

If this life is your first
this is all I can prescribe,
if this is number two or three
then you know more than I.

Trespassers Going Home

The cats in our backyard are lean & scrawny
They trespass without guilt and go home
to a favorite corner
of a favorite room.

They leave us to die in a thousand battles
yet
they stumble back:

starved, defeated, and they lie down
at our feet like drowned men
washed upon shore.

90 degrees

The doors are propped open with
portable fans
which blow hot air through the house
and all but sing doing so.

The fuschia– limp in its hanging basket
on the front porch
bleeds its hot pink & red blossoms onto
the cool black wrought-iron grillwork.

Inside, the afternoon sun is orange
through my orange curtains.

The Boston fern hangs heavy & lush
from the ceiling hook
and it feeds on the torpid air with
green sighs.

My cats sleep an exhausted sleep–
dream steamy feline dreams– & wake
with the jungle in their eyes.

If

If my eyes were as green & clear as
my cat's eyes
emerald, seductive, mysterious...
all women would envy me.

If my skin was as smooth as
hers is silky-sable,
men would line up just for a chance
to stroke me.

If my life was as simple and uncomplicated
as hers
I'd be content with a warm shaft of sunlight
on cool linoleum floors,

spend hours entranced with a bit of string;
live each day to the fullest

with no thought, nor care
for what tomorrow brings.

In This Old House

In this old house for all we know
These rooms once held ladies frail and old
Who stayed inside avoiding snow
Who wrapped themselves against the cold
You'd even see them bundled up in spring
As if the slightest chill to their arthritic bones
Would give birth to a terminal fever and bring
The country doctor in his buggy far from home.
I know it was they who painted the windows closed
Lest their lungs breathe in the slightest draught of air
I know they boarded up the chimney, hid the nail holes
So afraid they were of burglars entering there.
I work all day to pry the windows open
But quietly... I wouldn't want the ghosts of tenants past to waken.

In Mornings When I Stagger From Our Room

In mornings when I stagger from our room
And turn and glimpse your steady breathing there
Your vulnerability, like a second moon,
Seems incongruous, hanging so obliquely in the air.
As you should know, I guess I will confess
It's not for supple strength I love you so
But for your easy show of tenderness
Unlike so many other men I've known.
If you should wake and catch me standing here
So awkward in my rumpled sleeping gown
I'd say "coffee's coming shortly," loud and clear
And hurry from the room, my head flung down
Lest you should see my face, the little tear
I'd run and wipe the traces, check the mirror.

Two Lives

When we at end of day in silence lie
Dressed for sleep yet naked on our bed
Recall the day's events, the long goodbye
Before we each in turn turn 'way our heads
Prepared for separate dreams we sweetly go
Into the long unconsciousness of night;
The landscapes we inhabit differ so
There's no defense against the spider's bite.
 A dream because it's so is no less real
Than all the circumstantial acts of day
We live two lives, two lives we breathe and feel
In one we pay for bread and our mistakes;
But in our lives at night upon our beds
We pay with dark long solitude instead.

The Flag

The flag that Betsy Ross so deftly spun
Beside the oil lamp embroidering
Has now to me a mockery become.
The red stripes bleed into the blue it seems
As if the laundry wasn't separated right,
Or maybe bleach was added by mistake
Or someone mixed the colors with the whites.
This is the flag I often will forsake
Like a lover who has gone not to return.
When our brothers reluctantly should fight
Some Asian country only to be spurned
By those who praise the symbol of the Right,
It's time to reassess those stripes and stars
And in her name stop going off to wars.

To Kim

When all is said and done and you must go
And I must stay behind and bake the bread
And air the sheets upon my marriage bed
I hope that you'll not envy me my home
Or husband, cats, or lawn that's newly mown.
Upon the road I hope you're always fed
That you'll not tire of living or praise the dead;
I hope when lonely, you are not alone
I hope that you're warm when winter winds are freezing
I wish you well in all you wish to do
May strangers on the highway remain kind
I hope your days of sorrow all are few
That what you seek, you in your seeking find.

Blackberries

In summer when the days are hot & long
I go out in the yard my tools in tow
To weed out foliage which does not belong
Like the blackberry clutching tight to grow & grow.
It reaches heights unmerciful, I think
The roots and stems grow equally awry,
And when I pause to take a thirsty drink,
I swear it's grown another arm to sky.
The thorns bite at my pruning shears
And branches bend to prick my little hands;
This berry that has grown for years and years
Rebels draws blood leaves scratches on my arms.
But in the mornings, jam upon my bread,
This enemy I have battled is now sweet, so sweet
Delicious and red.

First Flight

While there is sunlight in the brief days passing
And spring is written in the pale blue sky
With cream puff clouds in the heavens massing
And gawky fledglings fall from nests to fly
Without a worry of the rocky ground below
While mother birds attend to things they do
This time of year their patience I extoll.
As they survey this aerial debut
Of babes they warmed when in the shell to hatch
And worms they stole dropped struggling into beaks
How they never left the nest nor broke the watch
Til they heard the first dry hungry shrieks
And so it is each spring some leave the nest
And some survive and some are not so blessed.

Sonnet For A Bored Housewife

Your being there is just a pantomime
You get up in the morning 'cause you must
You wash the dishes, sweep the floors and dust.
Marriage is your pastime and your crime;
He robbed you neatly, left no trace behind.
That two should live together first in lust
Then eat the bread of love and leave just crust
Does more harm than the ravages of time.
So if he proposes marriage on his knee
Because he loves you for your fragile things,
Beware of his designs for robbery:
Lock your dearest treasures, hide the key
Then and only then reply, yes-yes
For love is just a bargain at its best.

Love's Season

The summer sun shows no remorse
The heat makes steel to slacken
The river, having run its course,
Is gone but for the bracken.
    The heated globe that is my heart
Has seasons of its own;
It stirs within me, is a part
Of all the earth has ever known.
    This summer, love, my heart is high
It thumps so quick upon my breast
Til winter's long, dark alibi
In cold forbidding truth is dressed.
Til then, til then, embrace me dear,
Summer comes but once I fear.

Your Grandfather's Eyes

I pretend not to see your grandfather's eyes
In his goldleaf portrait on the wall
His piercing expression, stern and wise
Thru amber glass observe us as we fall
Nakedly in some obscene embrace
Our arms and legs thrown here and there
With brazen erotica we climb to satiate
The final curve our bodies make I know
The effort's worth this moment that we share
And I pretend not to see your grandfather's eyes
Twinkle for a moment in voyeuristic sighs.

Captive - a sonnet

Oh come now let me not repass
These ugly woods that hold me captive nigh.
Their gnarled branches pray a deathly mass
In cloaks of moss and rot convincingly.
I used to love the bird, the squirrel at play;
These also mock and chant, and taunt me so,
I pray the soggy pulpit of the Jay
Would tumble down; turn mute; and leave me go.
     Arise the super-stores, the neon lights,
The crowds of people... faces everyone
That speak my tongue, though maybe not precise.
We'd have a carnival, balloons & so much fun,
perhaps I'd even find the secret stair...
A neighbor in for tea– a way from here to there.

Johny Blue-Eyes

Yesterday the murderer was caught
In a rented room somewhere downtown.
For many months he had been sought
For the deaths of seven women, mostly young.
Police had interviewed his many friends
Who'd known him from a very early age
"He was a model student" they all said,
Was captioned 'neath his smile on the front page.
I'd always pictured killers with dark eyes
And burley arms– hair sprouting from their hands
As outcasts in alleys clutching knives
Look-a-like Quasimodos hiding behind garbage cans.

But, Johny now at night I will beware
Of pretty blue-eyed boys, sweet smiles, fair hair.

Sleep's Gift

At night I lay me down to sleep
'Neath floral sheets fresh and clean
Smoke my last cigarette, count the sheep
Douse the lights– my last routine
And know somewhere some beggar lies
On a cold straw mat, on a cold dirt floor
Who was never weaned on lullabies
Who asks for dreams and nothing more;
While elsewhere in satin-canopied beds
Toss and turn the pampered rich
On goosedown pillows they lay their heads
While their bodies, from too much brandy, twitch.
I pity the pauper, the rich even more;
Sleep's gift is for the deserving, regardless of decor.

If You Could Love Me Less

If you could love me less, my feelings more
The time it matters not, nor life's surcease
As we are shipwrecked lovers on this shore
Our enmity at times it may increase.
But who's to say love's doomed to fade with years
Or that familiarity breeds contempt?
We've been together not without our fears
And if you doubt my sincerity, praise the attempt.
In marriage mother's gentle hand we lose
Upon our fevered foreheads late at night,
Your kisses often leave a little bruise
But I know they're born of love, so that's all right.
I f I could love you less, your feelings more
I'd say let's try again and close the door.

When I Am Gone And Mossy Death Shall Claim Me

When I am gone and mossy death shall claim me
And as I'm poor there'll be no tombstone there
No fluted angel bragging on my grave to see
Just rock and weeds, no epitaph will I bear.
For the dead in shallow graves, lips turned to stone
Had their chance in life to speak their say.
No thin bronze prose can immortalize bone
So speak out, let your voice be heard today.
Silent is the mouth when closed forever
We all one day are creatures deaf and dumb
The dead return to haunt nobody ever
Tis a rumor begun by clever mediums.
So if I'm gone and you should hear my voice
It will not be of my doing, but your choice.

The Empty Refrigerator

This is not a poem about poverty
though surely one more wouldn't
hurt

but rather about being poor

about questions without answers
which fill our lives
like books in perpetual encyclopedia

and leave room for nothing else.

Electricity is a wonder
we cannot see

yet we worship the
small, dim bulb
in our bathrobe and slippers

and pray for a hotdog or candybar
before we shut the heavy door.

In the dark I stumble back to our sleeping
bed and you
hoping dreams alone might satiate

one night more.

Two Dreams on a Hot California Summer Day

Dust puffs
the color of dirty cotton candy
trailed from the tailpipe of the ancient Model-T
as it rumbled under the California
eucalyptus trees.

It huffed along like an emphysemic old man
and we sat inside her
me & you– a boy of eighteen,
a girl of ten
(me– dreaming we were married
            riding across the prairie
            in a western movie,
            Grace Kelly in High Noon
            elegant in green satin,
            Gary Cooper at the reins)

(you– hot from working in the scorching orchard
            with sweat stains damp continents under your arms–
            Africa on the right; Australia on the left)

All you could think of
was the beer in the icebox
so cold
it would hurt
going down.

Time

Alarmclocks:

the hands beat my brains out
years ago

the gongs on top which tortured are
broken
and clatter silently into the white
toilet bowl.

Time is flushed from my belly
like Jonah from the whale

leaving behind an empty room
full of roadmaps and seashells

while outside– under an ashen sky
some gamey rooster hobbles mute
and blind.

It was time alone that destroyed him,
I'll mutter,
and roll over in my ancient bed

feeling blameless
and victimized.

Poppies

Poppies grow wild in Turkey
blooming like red mouths
speaking to the sky.

Addicts grow wild in the city
having fallen asleep– like Dorothy–
once too often
in a field of flowers.

Poppies grow wild in the city
and they're so beautiful
that once you fall asleep
your dreams are so good

that you never want to wake.

American Blues

Crocheted pink turtle on the
edge of the bathtub
Mr. Microphone is soap on a rope

Write me a hit tune
to pay for the mortgage

I could be sailing down the Nile
on a lazy afternoon

Instead of having these
American Blues.

The Gambler

A roulette wheel in my frontal lobes
spins
in the Reno of my mind
where the winning word is
perfectly formed - from red rage
or black equanimity i cannot say

think I'll escape to the Tahoe of my dreams
where a lake bluer than promise
twinkles in the
wilderness from a plane

are you at the controls
harboring Piper Cub mentality?

Can you count the spots on a deer
with your smart binoculars?

Next year
I'll vacation further, even,
than the clothesline
in the backyard
Maybe gamble with a pair of crooked dice
on the kitchen floor

enter
my Las Vegas bathroom
with its overhead light my

hot pink neon fantasy zigzagging
off the double mirror

I'll dream of paradise
as I climb naked
into the risky bathtub

turn both faucets on full force.

The Apricot Orchard

Some lives are so empty and so shallow but
the apricot trees are in bloom and
two white horses with golden manes
preen in the sun.

They escaped from the circus
leaving behind a pretty girl in a short pink dress.
In lonesome arabesque
she cries and cries.

The apricots are bruised with ripeness
Sienna-colored seeds scatter along
the husky orchard rows.

It is high noon some people are so shallow/
The white horses are free / some people are so empty.

Feeding the Lions

I am a slave girl
being led to feed
the lions

           my aquamarine eyes ....my eyes......

The men hunger
after me.

Hercules' shield
is nowhere in sight...

The blonde woman
in the boxed stall
condemns my beauty

           my aquamarine eyes ....my eyes......

My hair is hot
under
a chestnut sun.

Self-Esteem

What I want to say is:
I need a new language to say this in;

Not that I love you,
you know that already

but that I wonder
what I'd do alone

without you propping me up
with contemporary jokes
and "Zest" washed flesh.

Self-esteem
is an invisible flutist
looking in the dormer window
who never plays.

I hear nothing
but the drip of the bathtub faucet
in an arid cool morning bathroom.

If At First You Don't Succeed

like the living air
going out of a balloon

we collapse all around us

and go on.

My Aquarium

The fish in my aquarium
must wonder why I stare at them
their little mouths are mouthing O's
gulping water as they go.

The lightbulb in my living room
is my fishes' sun and moon
when I go to bed at night
their sun sets quickly out of sight.

If only I could hold my breath
and shrink to just my fishes' width
I'd join them in their tiny sea
play chase around a fake palm tree.

We would swim through teeny castles
life would be without its hassles
but content to stare I'll be
til I grow gills or drown at sea.

Needlepoint

Crochet my hands in knots
Needlepoint my thumbs ablaze
Thread with a bloodshot eye
This needle I engage.

Making Dinner

I am left alone in the kitchen
To make dinner.
If I could only trade my wares
for Apollo's winged feet
or Joan of Arc's cross,
I would fly cleansed into the sun,
sing with angels thousand,
return
and gladly bake bread
for a million men.

A Poem to Ten-Year Old Dreamers

O, you silly puddle jumpers,
Snowman creators,
Sing in the wind worshippers
Of violent leaf falls
And tender blossomings…

You think you have the answer
In your morning cornflake prize.
O, I laugh not at your
Small wonders– you life creators,
Who do not care
For awkward intruders–
The obese lookers-on into your bubbled worlds.

Float East of the sun,
West of the moon, Give
The Snow Queen my regards,
Bring me a silver twig from
The land marooned under many rivers–

But heed.
Wise seekers.
That you do not repeat our sin.
Do not lose your golden slipper too soon.

Flight

I want to go– turn your face
and do not watch
me race
towards the brilliant night.
Baubles of colored light
will fold me into
my two-dimensional Oz...
And if you must follow
    Because
of too much caring,
promise not to take my hand,
laugh your eyes and understand
that all flight
is not sin.

Just Remembering

Just remembering
when Bob Dylan was our messiah
and drugs our panacea,
just recalling then.

Tearfully balanced on the axis
of tender worlds,
men wore our mysteries and
our hems were raised
like peacocks just for them.

Just remembering
when Hans Christian Anderson taught
us fantasy
in the wild and beautiful castles
of lost princes.

Then... hoping we were ready
for the throes of Russian poets,
Mother moved us on
as we bled with Dostoyevsky
in our dreams.

And remembering
schemes of things,
how we played with paper replicas
of genetics;
how we cherished our eager drawings
of crabs and seas and things.

Will Go

Will go,
press against the darkling membrane
pulsing through
the soft place of no shadows.

Drink blood,
sleep the ogres to death
hurl pastel boomerangs
into a waterless sea.

It's Raining and My Eyes are Wet Bertolt Brecht

It's raining and my eyes are wet, Bertolt Brecht.
I'm crying and I'm smiling Golden Boy.
      Tend your precious flowers,
      Die in some dark bower.
Power keeps me kept.

Sing inside a face, with every word a worried
face– straight lace–

I've prayed for those who've cared and never
sat upon a chair without composure.
I've grown my auburn hair, it can blow just anywhere
inside this windstorm.

Come tell me that I'm pretty, but not really very
witty–
      Pour crisp Corn Flakes in a bowl, and then I'll
really know I'm whole and you are holy.
      Yes, I'll know that I am whole
And you are holy.

Exit - To Prince

A crystal candelabra sighs in the room
with shut-eye doors.
The melons rock, uneaten, while
folks shout curses from all floors.

The suicide freeway streams under sky
I've found my way to the Southern Cross
I'll take flight number 205
I see the gilded airplane wing,
I color crayon on trays– people
bob to the champagne deck
with tilted glass and eyes.

A mist enshrouded Fiji beckons
marketeers everywhere– Ah to
buy some dire trinkets, I'll
wear them in my hair.

My prince has flown, I discover
as I land in Australia town
I see his empty castle
with wild flowers gone dead from
growing.

The fair King smiles - his rubies
flashing everywhere
He asks me where I come from
I say from over there.

He hands me a pearl ring
says my dreams will all come true

if I shear my hair
wear darkly capes and
pray for his vagabond son.

Answering - my home it moans to me
my dragonflies are lonely
Farewell O King, I'm going away
to seek the prince in London.

To Nureyev

Like a snake curved upon sand
I sunk against the
warm dunes of your body.

Warm sand sifted around
my arched neck and
my breast grew in the
caves of forgotten snakes.

Future

I heard a cry weak & throaty
as I sped the rushing air
of easy dreams.

"I beg you– break down these
concrete cities, with one blow
painlessly

We'll rebuild with sticks & stones
we'll breathe again
we'll breathe."

Earth 3000

In a quiet corner of never
this room is a paradox of geometry,
all boxey, no windows,
no catcalls here

Foliage is glass bottles
beakers of flowers, brittle nastertiums,
celluloid philodendrons.

You come from light years in time,
seconds from yesterday,
cherishing a climate of seasonal rain
and bronze tan summers.

As here there is no photosynthesis
and the men are as impotent as these
tired rooms. Today is nowhere to be.
In the year 3000.

I Would Bleed So Beautifully

I would bleed so beautifully
I would bleed a flower for every night
I slept in the garden of you

bleeding against all my purity

I would leave a scarlet rose between
white sheets
My room would fill up with wine
and casements of rich velvet

I would bleed
I would bleed so beautifully.

Teeter-Totter

My body could plunge
through clouds of
metaphysical teeter-tottering
and I would still remain
right-side up.

There and Back

Oh my God Oh my God
The slackening contours of people
shimmered in the yellow
light of early morning with
their screams stabbing the
quiet edges of my self.
A collage of naked ladies
balancing on the corner
table took young boys
to sin and back
while my arms beckoned
them to me.
My hands kept reaching out
but fell into a treadmill
turning always in the same dream.
The bars of the short blue chair
supported my balloon mind which
had forgotten the
triangular arch of his
body.

On Opening and Closing Doors

I tried to form a wall of glass.
You know – the kind I can
Look out, but no one breathing 'round
May look in.
The me inside myself
Let out strings of marionettes
I told them what to say,
But as days passed
They tilted their wooden faces
To the moon– laughed out loud to boot
And became independent
When my back was turned.
On their first 4th of July they
Let me play and we
Filled the sky with eight different smiles
And we each had our own way
Of throwing color.
You stood outside my wall
And played games and
Named us all.
But you had to walk away
When I decided not to play,
Grew weary laughing;
Left my dolls to dance
Under the sun,
Unheeded by anyone.

African Dream

Deep in the heart, deep in the heart
of Africa.
Foliage grows through my ears
I hear water bubbling at my feet
I see my heart pierced with native ivory
I feel lions heaving circular manes.
I know I am lost
I am lost deep in the heart
deep in the heart of Africa.

There Is A Shadow

There is a shadow
which follows me;
I feel like Peter Pan
as I go humping from room to room.

In my dreams I go flying
over housetops
to crocodile summers
and cool lagoons

(It has no preference for sun or moon)

There is a shadow
which follows me.
But it is only my past
nailed to my heels
by the crude carpenter of memory.

I stumble and fall.
It's hard to walk for two.

Gov-Mart Bazaar

10 pak 37¢ – the best
candy on Earth comes
from…
>   last night has not
>   dissolved today
>   I walk, I talk
>   I'm kool-pops
>   (freeze and eat me
>   anytime)
But thaw me when
the checkers go home
and curl bargains under their toes.

* * *

Piquantly devour the
cellophaned hamburger
snug in wrapped grocery packages.
Climb into the steel cart
and disappear.

Og

In a cavern dark and eerie
Sat a man who never wearied.

While he sat,
He pondered fiercely,
Pondered in the cave quite fiercely.

Then an axe, all bright and gleamy,
Caught his eye, ever gleaming.

On that night of caves and darkness,
There arose an awful rumbling.

Not, of darkness
Did the bellow
Of the land from out that cavern
Reach his ear,
and– thus– his eye,
While he mightily
Touched the yellow

Sword he made that night.

Run

Run, there is no other word but run.
Run without glancing at curious faces
Or painted grocery stores.
Run through and through the
Dollish-town, through men who ask
You what you hope to find.
Run past interrogators, past
Everyone's imaginary tortoise,
Past your own consciousness.

Alice

O, Alice, Alice why do you grow so tall?
And play croquet and dine delightfully
And attend a real queen's ball?

O, Alice, Alice tell me of your land
Where rabbits chase and turtles sigh
And caterpillars smoke opium.

O, Alice, Alice where are you now?
Blue-frocked, goldilocked, knowing
All there is to know.

Babylon

Where would you be at the
end of the world?
Would you sit and comfort me?
The word is out
We'll all snuff out
in a week or two or three.

Would you sit all alone
in your one-room room,
Would you drink till you
couldn't see?
Would you mind if I sat
outside your door
and listened to you breathe?

Before I come sit beside your door
I'll prepare myself like a nun.
(saying my rosary constantly)
I'll cut my hair– grown so long.

I'll lay my hair in a sequined case
and bathe in oil of jasmine,
I'll dress in pale Spanish lace
and not forget my talismans.

Can't you just see us sitting there
on either side of that fabled door
waiting for evermore?

You know,
that door was there before.

There is an Old Man

There is an old man who eats
garbage out of trash cans
across from Freidlander & Sons.

They keep the diamonds locked up
at night, lest no one steal
What they do not own.

The Umbrella

this broken umbrella
a few spokes stuck like bird bones
jab through the red nylon cloth
ready for Goodwill's drop-off box
Shields me almost from the sleety rain
& menacing wind on the concrete sidewalk
Broken by a wrenching wind turned inside out
almost carrying me aloft as its back broke.

View From An Open Window In Fremont

Windchimes, miniature blue & pink
Chinese pagodas, chink – plink
and sway on my back porch
Near bamboo curtains.

They move in the white-blue,
almost still air of spring.

Above the chimes the Aurora Bridge–
monumental– concrete grey
abuts this subtle landscape.

An occasional pedestrian
is silhouetted crossing the bridge.
The cars are few,
It's Sunday after all...

and my cats are sleeping.

St. Vinnies

Old baby cribs sit here and there
peeling paint in the open air,
rusty throw-aways beyond repair...

The Betty Crocker silverware
bought with coupons saved for years
rattles in an open bin
while I pause and rifle through them.

Royal blue Noxema jars
remind me of my teenage years;
They catch the light while
Mother Mary tall and bright
guards the entrance on my right.

O' I am mighty cautious
under her plaster eye

Who knows how long those dresses there
will gather dust in this open air;
hand-me-downs are handed over,
a pretty dress for just a dollar.

St. Vincent in your legacy
I wonder if you'd foreseen
this pitiful second-hand
cemetary...

Things we kill
but never bury.

Downtown Seattle at Night

The evening is a valentine
arms around the moon,
a black velvet curtain
enfolds us in its arms.

The drunks are out and down
in doorways of the city,
nursing Thunderbird in paper sacks
like mothers with their babies.

Their hollow eyes
beseech the night
for shelter from the storm
(their brothers back in Omaha
would die to see them so).

At dusk their ragged features fade
and fold into the night;
a little drink to kill the pain
and everything's alright.

Two Photographs

Sitting in a wooden straight backed chair
(her hair a brown cushion through the slats)
my grandma sipped coffee, mud black
and looked like a photograph that
Weston might have caught
alongside the
bell pepper
and chambered nautilus.

Ansel Adams' "Moonrise Over Hernandez" was
her favorite print and she watched its stark
skies for a sign or a savior but it never came.

The moon looks through her threadbare lace
curtains, through the kitchen window shines
a cone-shaped clown's light

(its pattern through the ecru crochet
is testament to what her mother had to give)

She says tomorrow is just a ruffle of air,
tintype of the wind,
for all that matters.

Geranium Summer

Goodbye goodbye geranium summer
they've found opium poppies
in the south of the city

turn your head, turn your head
see the downtrodden
sweet-black and oily
flowers that we reap.

Goodbye goodbye geranium summer
sweet pink and spiky
it sucks out the pain.

Goodbye goodbye geranium summer
sweek black and oily
it sucks out the hate.

Goodbye goodbye geranium summer
they've found opium poppies
in the south of the city

turn your head, turn your head
see the downtrodden
sweet black and oily
flowers that we reap.

Carnival

Someone's ex-wife shuffles cards
on the half-moon counter
of her glass ticket cage.

A city cowboy strikes up a coversation
with a set of bowling pins
while the barker's in the back
filling them with lead.

Cotton candy rises like a chorus
of pink clouds
above the blonde curls
of a sea of children

While an over-ripe girl
in a slit skirt
sells dollar kisses
in a heart-shaped booth.

Along the midway
the hammer drives its victims
into the ground
over and over again
as the ferris wheel
suspends teenage lovers in an arc of magic
on the whispering air.

At closing time the carnival lights
bracelet the night
with a million precious stones

and fake fur monkeys ride their wooden sticks
all the way home.

Puyallup Fair

except for the worst burgers
we'd ever eaten
it was a good day

i think the burgers were
cooked at least a couple of hours
before we arrived

left to get cold then
re-heated in a microwave
at which time over-cooked onions
like slug entrails were added.

cheese? just barely.
and the buns had to be day-old.

But the sheep exhibit later
made up for it
their faces looked like
they'd been cut out of
white/or black felt and stuck in place

there's not much to say about
the sheep
just that they tried to converse with
awkward bleats in their clean pens
heaped with straw;
that the secondhand water ran into
floor drains from the
sloping cement floors.

248

or that blue ribbons rose in the eyes
of farm girls as they clipped & patted;
carded & combed

as their reluctant sheep were held
immobile
in crude looking head pieces.
(rustic sheep braces?)

Baby strollers led eager parents
from stall to stall &
outside, on the promenade,
a million pair of acid-washed jeans walked in
twos & threes.
Their owners hair was mostly long & blonde
& crimped,
victim of the latest appliance
(waffle iron for hair)
Will that be a light, medium or dark crimp?

Then we rode the skyride.
Couldn't help but gaze nonstop at the
delicate-looking pulley system
I was about to entrust with the
remainder of my life

figured the odds were against
my immediate death
never-the-less
chose "one-way" rather than "round trip"

& was too scared to peer down & out at the
view I'd just paid to get.

Got off...
was nearly late afternoon.
It seemed wherever we walked the sun was
in our eyes.
(Thought I truly understood the meaning
of crowd-swell

Shoulder to shoulder isn't
quite accurate enough...
more like cheek to jowl,
or– to be more precise–
kneecap to groin.)

You see why I love crowds
Why I can't wait til next year
to do it all over again.

Masterpiece

The swinging saloon door
opens into the mirrored bar
where a naked lady
in her gold edged frame reposes

above rows of whiskey bottles.
(She favored Kentucky bourbon
straight
up
and giggled after just one swallow)

Her arms and legs
are blue in their whiteness
but there is a high blush
of color
above each breast.

Mistress of gunfighters & kings;
breasts, arms, lips, thighs,
we salute her...
mistress of us all...

and order another round.

Ex-Smoker

I miss the lavender clouds
of drifting smoke
the long, deliberate inhalation;
the perfect smoke signals sent up like
an Indian arching his blanket
over an open fire.

I miss the play of match and cigarette,
the kiss of the filtertip;

the smoke rings
sailing halfway across the room
advertising tombstones.

Something More

Do we want
something nobler than this?
The handsome young man
in his BMW,
the Pacific ocean riding over his shoulder,
carrot juice drinks,
skies bluer than madness,
White teeth
reflecting abundant good health.

Symphonies that would make Beethoven cry
orchestrate our hero's journey
towards what is supposed to be
what we desire most
a swimming pool in Beverly Hills,
clean, bright children.
cool drinks aflair with circles of lime
are sipped
under candy-striped backyard awnings.

We are important in our automobiles.
We go round and round the same tracks.
On our cellular phones
we push buttons with authority
and faith.

Rock 'N Roll Dusk

In the failing light
sunsets drift over smoky towns
as our days wind down.

The hollow call of childhood
whistles thru our thumbs
the summer sidewalks are warm
under bare feet
cracks ripple in the concrete,
someone pulls his blinds down.

Rock 'n Roll lulls us to
a frenzy on car stereos all over town

Mustangs cruise First Street
looking for whores
Fords go through car washes
shaped like elephants;
VW vans barrel along
carrying no-nonsense women.

A pink sky engulfs us
without a sound.

Epithet

We are experiencing technical difficulties
t.v. is a slice of moon
newsreels haven't improved even with living
color.
its gray on gray
we are conditioned not to see
the blood speck in the eye of the announcer:
admit to red, bend to blue–
adjust the fine tune.

Farenheit 451 has come true
coffee tables are bare of magazines
people don't read anymore, Architectural
Digests are stuffed in garbage cans
after the lid is pried off

they won't read this   either.

Tenement

I sat on the stairs
my heart was thumping
my knees drawn up real close
I was trying to be as
small as possible

I hoped no one would come
I hoped no one would ask me questions
I hoped I wouldn't cry
& my knees rode my chest even tighter

I heard a door open
It was a loud opening
I didn't look to see
but I knew it was my door

I didn't know who came out
Did my Daddy kill my Mommy
Did my Mommy kill my Daddy
Who won?

The Antique Shop

As I enter
a tinny bell sounds a rusty ding-a-ling.
Everything is carefully arranged;
the room smells like summer attics
and musty velvet pillows.

The room is crammed with bureaus
polished with Old English lemon oil;
Here– an ornate pink and gold hairbrush
and handmirror
(I see a 19th century woman brushing
her long heavy hair)
There– a porcelain pitcher and water basin
(I see the same woman washing and daubing
her body with rosewater, a body no one,
not even her husband, sees).

There are boxes of old photographs, tintypes
of prim, beautiful women with elaborate
hairdos wearing high lace collars;
anonymous infants in baptism gowns;
a family of five all looking stern and
somber for the camera
    All are dead– saved in no one's family album.

Maxfield Parrish prints line the walls:
Ideal girls, barely dressed,
posed perched on rocks against an
unreal blue sky.

I finger the rusted tin containers
which once held saltines or baking soda
and know that I have no use for them
even if they are unique and
might look arty on my windowsill.

I touch all the bits and pieces
of people's lives
(here and there on display)
and suddenly feel like an intruder
and I know for certain
that when I leave
the door will shut
with a rusty ding-a-ling behind me.

Downtown Seattle and The Library at Noon

Gulls "skree" and "skaw", whoop and dive
between ebony skyscrapers
and frenzy for first dibs on cheeseburger
crumbs and french fries.

Pedestrians jostle for first place
at stop lights then jockey for position
in long cafeteria lines.
Gray-suited men with black attaché cases
carry folded newspapers under their arms
while their secretaries, slim and blonde,
go slumming in the public market and detest
the pigeons.

The dinosaur bones in front of Sea-First are
bronze and beautiful in the noon light
and out of place.
Across the street at the public library, many,
like me,
wait for the midday doors to open.

It is Thursday
We each plan our day's itinerary and grow restless
waiting.

Years ago I'd head for the music floor
and cry along with Mimi in La Boheme...
(Puccini alive again in the soundproof
rooms)

Students of business still crowd the second floor
desks. Furiously bent over economic texts,
they memorize theory with button-down monotony.

It used to be o.k. to smoke in the reading room
but this attracted the wrong sort
who'd fall asleep in the leatherette chairs
and dream they were already home, curled up
with a good book beside a raging fire.

Sweepstakes

I would phone up
all five of my neighbors
simultaneously

and say to each of them
at the same time

"You have just won
one million dollars"

Then I'd sit low
in my Studebaker

and watch the faces
of all five
as they stumbled out
their front doors.

Virginia

She stood there large and alone.
Wearing her white parade-marching
Uniform, milky in the evening sun.
She nudged a square hand into
The pit of a gold-tassled pocket
and shuffled a dandelion flower
From a broken cement crack.

No one felt her "look at me's"
But I,
Watching from my kitchen window,
Sadly remembering her stolid pride
Telling me of golden horns
And practiced, polished boots
Soon to march in the Seafair parade;
Of the beautiful belonging.

Kansas in Seattle

Kansas comes tossing back,
burning through the
sweet dry grass
along the lake.
I imagine years of sunflowers
carelessly maturing,
sidling away from the wind,
blowing warm topaz seeds
into wind-eroded crevices.

Eastlake Route to Town

Worn Coca-Cola signs and wizened apples
timidly adorn the front of
tumbledown shops.
The trolley bus rattles on,
past the squat Chinese laundries, and
I wonder
whose white shirts are being carefully
starched, and I wonder if the smiling doll-like
man
will eat enough tonight.

The trolley passes more shops, more
aproned men and women standing in
the bleak doorways of their lives
waiting for someone, someone who might
need bread or a pound of instant coffee.

The bus teeters to a stop and
I run up the brick sidewalk
past the Chinese laundries,
and
buy three apples and a coke.

The Tavern

You rationed praise with the stinginess
of a starving pioneer parcelling out
jerky at Donner Pass

even though I danced for you
in a cotton skirt on a table top
of wooden planks and glass

even though a pool hustler leaned on his cue
then looked up my dress
before looking at you.

I decided it was time to go home
when a barmaid named Stardust
thumbtacked my shadow to the loghewn wall,
bowling trophies, elkhorn, beernuts, all.

The Office

Like trained bears
all the secretaries
do tricks all day long or so.
Some type with their tits
some perform fellatio.

Their neckchains are
cool snakes made of real gold
they clink and tangle over
self-corrected memos fed to their
pastel typewriters.

And you, as boss, watch
from your glass wall, and let out a burp
as your hands tame your lap

You are very pleased with yourself.

Dorian Gray

I wish I had a portrait in the attic
intact with all the blight and wit of years
A handsome face gone strained around
the edges
what matter if from laughter or from tears.

The half-truths -maybe even if not lies-
begin to show around the painted eys
the snaking lines like rays about the lips
betray the anger spent
and love's sweet kiss.

but, as it is the canvas isn't there
I wear it nakedly for all to see
Some say we all deserve the face we get
and factor not the uphill battles won
the etching path of life's own brutal brush
the tug and pull of joy and tragedy.

Homeless

Outside the courthouse at four-o-five
in the darkening afternoon
Already a few of the homeless
are staking their claims
for a place to spend the night.

A concrete, recessed window ledge
is invitation to a bundle of tattered
blankets... a shopping bag or two.

Already, one man is asleep (I presume)
From here– across the street– the
nearly imperceptible fall and rise of
his body can be seen.

I think of a beached whale dying its
huge death on a cold northern shore.

Occasionally, I glimpse a man's hand
emerge from his self-made tent to beg
a cigarette or quarter from office
workers on their way home.

What? No pillow. No warmth against
this ragged February wind...

Hope dies.

The Other Side of the City

The other side of the city means your house.
I can almost see you lying behind your green shutters.
The other side of the city crouches beneath Capitol Hill.
You stride down to Lake Union and watch the water;
You sit on your own vacant dock.
The other side of the city is
Landscapes I will never paint,
Rain I will never prepare for,
You.
And I believe it is the other side of the world.

Sunday Afternoon

Capitol Hill pulses with lights like the
Body of a wakened spider.
The mountains rise after a good rain,
And telephone poles walk
Clear into town.
Christmas gone,
New Year's not quite here,
I spend my afternoons not reading
Everything I was going to read,
Being graced with procrastination.

Dust

In this house
Nothing grows
But dust on the floor.

It doubles and triples in corners
Feeding on fallen hair
And muddy boot droppings.

It evades my dustpan;
takes flight on my broom.
It lifts off the runway of the floor
And
    in little clouds, h-o-v-e-r-s.

There are no crash landings.
Only fluttering whispers of descent
Into some unreachable place.

I am useful.
Some days my broom and I spend hours
Chasing down the enemy.

The Dentist

The room is small and over-lit.
I sit in the yellow recliner
with octopus arms
one arm holds slim sterile picks
another holds drills which look
like miniature jackhammers.

I wait forever for the dentist
and study the frosted glass ceiling and
the carefully selected abstract paintings
on the wall;
I listen to Muzak coming from
invisible speakers.

At last the dentist comes
and I study his well-groomed fingernails
(immaculate with nails clipped short)
and I'm so lost in the clean, sweet smell
of his shirt
that I hardly notice
the prick of the needle going in
    the long
             dull pain after.

Clocks, & Bells, & Buses

Your groggy smile & tousled hair
is charming in the morning, dear.
When I come to wake you up– I smile
while setting down your coffee cup
and just before you wake & say I love you
I kiss your sleeping face.

The clocks & bells & buses though
are there commanding me to go.
I rush past you and sometimes grumble,
and raffle through my closet clothes.
I dress & cuss & curse the time
It's off to work and out the door.

The telephones at work– ring– ring
and there's coffee for a sleepy staff to brew.
It's type & dash & type & dash...
but surely though I'll stop at noon
and think inside– I love you
                    I love you

If sometimes... this stranger me,
should hurry so & ramble that
I never seem to really say (outloud) I love you–
I'm just sorry that the clocks & bells & buses
sometimes talk louder than I do.

Marathon

The world running too fast
for dreamers,
will one day find itself
alone.

In Transit

Slumbering along
into the rushing night,
this bus echoes only the sound of air
and brakes afright.

It moves through a slate-gray light
beyond dusk
into the shadow the moon makes.

Red and green lights are strung
like Christmas globes.
They sway from their cables
like scarlet & emerald strobes.

In transit is suspension
out of control–
I am hypnotized and breathless
as I pay my fare and go.

A Slow Day At The Office

The glass frog on my desk is full of pens
all waiting to write something urgent & essential.
My in basket is empty
And the out basket has been clear 3 days now.
The telephone with 4 incoming lines keeps me busy though.

Lost Job

On the davenport I sit all day
Thinking of the office jobs I've lost
From going neatly & efficiently insane,
And you'd never guess the pity that it cost.
It started when I began omitting dates
On important memos going out
And then one morning I came in late
And cried when my boss began to shout.
And then my fingers forgot the typing keys,
My voice would tremble on the phone.
I decided it was time to pack and leave
When the office knew all the secrets of my home.
This would all be so embarrassing to recall
If it weren't so sad remembering my fall.

Dusk

Glint sun and
feathery water lie
juxtaposed
securely in the
innermost
core of sky.

Piercing arrows of dying sunlight
protrude
between dense buildings
to shatter
the remaining fragments
of day.

Thoughts in a Crowded Room

People
funny people
I am one of them
I am
<u>that</u> person
walking down the street
or
<u>that</u> human
mingled in the crowd.

I am
<u>that</u> puppet
lined up against the
dark wall of the world
waiting...
with the rest.

Individual minds
do not exist
They are of no use.
Puppets
aren't supposed to think–
It is against nature.

A Laundromat Is

rows of washing
machines
with their greedy
tongues out

they subsist
on a diet of
quarters & dimes

their chugging
bellies
digest t-shirts
& jeans

and everything...
comes out clean.

Bus Ride in the Rain

Rain jerks like parameciums
on the bus window made of
spun sugar
and I trace the life of each
into spilling oblivion.

The metallic boundaries of the
window cool my forehead
feverish from the warm breath
of commuters– who sit and
read of suicides and labor
union disputes.

The Zoo

Soft wind today
allows the city to rest
on Earth.
The zoo holds a cornucopia
of people
flowing like fruit from
the straw corners
of the city, supposedly
here to see new
animals,
But I know
they only come
to see new people.

Diamonds

They dazzle in
the showcased
jeweler's hand.
From newlywed
to widow
diamonds are everything
there is to wish for.

Look! There goes
a river of jewels
through Johannesburg
bound for home;
blue-black miners
pick rock in National Geographic.

They are buried alive
for our greed
of the brilliant (goddamned) stones.

Rio Wenatchee

White-blossomed trees populate Wenatchee
with a canopy of bloom.
Migrant farmers and their children
mingle with ladders and
pick apples heavy on their stems.

These swift-footed runners;
swimmers of the Rio Grande
pass news of the North
like batons
back to their native land.

They live out of tin cans,
wear out cheap shoes,
Their faces bake prematurely beneath
a piteous sun.

The farmer sees only the long dark braid
down Rosita's back, moving like a slick snake
among the green leaves, heavy and black.

The farmer plays with his chin
thinking what a fine dollar it will bring
when the season ends.

Greece

We would eat ripe black olives
right off the trees
amidst small goat herds.

We would sit on sun-warmed rocks
overlooking the stark blue Aegean sea
flanked by sea birds.

We would lay seige to one another
in the shadow of an ageless
pillar upon some rocky crag...

Afterwards, in a cool, stone house,
we would sample exotic foods wrapped
in grape leaves,
nibble baklava dripping with honey
and sip dark, sweet Greek coffee
until the stars came out
in the still Homeric sky.

Fiji

Ebony shark fins
were small sails
circling the harbor

Mother and I bartered
with natives;
beads for my dresses

We were pulled
under a table
by a frantic shopkeeper

A policeman
stood in the doorway
in a white scalloped skirt

He boomed
"trading's illegal"
but we were well hidden

Fiji—
when I remember you
I think of those damn blue beads

melting coral dye
all down the front
of my best white dress.

India

color
smell —
sound
sensory

New Delhi–
land of carmine caste marks on
the foreheads of veiled women
with beautiful eyes–

(the double row of their eyelashes
traps the stones you throw their way.)

Endless steel rails split
the continent into ragged lies,
    the monsoon is so heavy with rain,
    the air grows old.

There is a drought in Bangalor
where the veiled women
with beautiful eyes
join a funeral party and throw pink
streamers on the open fires.

Hiroshima

cauliflower morning...
landscape with
its breath sucked out

Oh God...
a hand says
reaching toward the sky from
a crack in broken concrete

Enola Gay.
Who remembers your
name?

one pilot gone mad

A country
apologetic with shame...

Who split the atom?
Who backs away from survivors
with their torn skin?

A cloud mushrooms in pockets of
my brain.

Your legacy
looms over us
puts us to bed at night

(justifies, justifies).

Aftermath

There is no prayer-song in Lebanon
No choir of chosen angels
to tread the sunny sands in search of peace.

    A crazed terrorist
    lies dead
    among the innocent
        and
    Billy is sent home
    and all that's left
    are his arms and teeth

In the kibbutz
children learn to shoulder rifles
before they learn to spell the words
of war:
    N-E-G-O-T-I-A-T-I-O-N
is a lie
written in boys' ashes
on every wall.

No bird sits in the almond tree.

Giza Revisited, 1974 AD

Khufu, three thousand years ago,
You reigned as Pharaoh.
Condemning one million souls
To slave for you,
> your pride,
> and greed;
but I care not Khufu, for
You left your work upon history.

Proud Cheops stands as mighty now
And men as you still prophesy war.
My country's lost one million souls
To live one life,
> for the good
> and bad;
But I care not, Khufu, for
Your stone entrances modern men.

Khufu, scribes claim you wicked,
Selfish, and bound...
But, what you did to leave your mark
Upon lone earth evermore,
Would cast its spell for centuries more.

But I care not, Khufu,
I, too, dream of red stone...
Not you.

For in your deeds, and…deaths in time,
You left a monument, indelibly bold,
To lure and fancy
The common man.

And I care, yes, Khufu,
for never shall be another as you.
Yes, never shall be another you.

Someday

Someday when we have all said our
apologies for wrongs committed
against our fellow man, when we
have all said a final grace at the
bountiful table

someday when we have gone beyond
waiting for a better stage to act
upon, I will know you then– a
survivor of this world and my love

I will say prayers for you at this
autumn table, I will clasp your
hand at the foggy moonlit sunset;
we will gaze on endangered species
of birds and let them be our
honored guests

at the table of our regret... we will
lay down our lives for just an
instant and we will praise the
burnished change in each others
eyes and

wait for a brighter tomorrow in a
world of swan-filled ponds and
serene ebb tides.

Ground Zero

Out on a Sunday drive
at ground zero
and we know without saying
that Trident is somewhere
out at sea;

that the beautiful Ohio
is steaming her way into
the peaceful suburb
of Bangor, Washington

which was recently built up.
(Jack-in-the-Box and McDonalds
take the place of thistle-filled
meadows &

Midwestern engineers and their
corn-fed families
only grow healthier
on fresh air and cheeseburgers.)

Out on a Sunday drive
at ground zero
heading home after counting half a dozen
dilapidated barns, gray, defying gravity,
with our exposed film rolling in the glove
compartment.

and we know without saying
that the beautiful Ohio is steaming
her way into Bangor
and that soon all this will be only

a small red whisper from
the mouth of a
burned child:

"Seattle."

Prayer

Is my prayer an empty echo
in the night?
My fingertips tremble
as they seek to touch

Oh God, are you mother father
brother sister lover friend.
What language do you speak?
What have I done that
you remain unseen?

Myself, I would willingly
supplicate…lay prostrate
on the polished floor
like a novitiate taking
her final vow

if only you would
appear briefly.

A mountain is only a mountain.

I know planets revolve perfectly
in the endless heavens

I know miracles abound,
cells divide,
bees amaze,
flowers of a thousand kinds
say yes yes yes

Yet I ask
Yet I seek
Yet I homeward yearn

For Jesus at Easter

Christ in the garden
must have been brave
to clasp his hands and pray
into the black of blackest nights
while there was soot upon the roses
and not one soul believed him
not even old wise Moses
now turned cold as stone
in his old grave.

His healings, yes, were showy,
that's all anyone can say
and though the crowd just "ate em up"
the night still grew black as black
and his prayers
which echoed back to back
became both fierce and calm.

I know you've seen the picture
hanging in my Grandma's bedroom:
The shaft of light upon the rock,
The man himself in ragged prayer
beseeching with his tortured hands
for anyone to hear.

And though he, himself, believed
the night itself forgot
and now the garden's just some vacant lot
long since overgrown with weeds.

Circus

On a vacant lot their tent is raised
In the poorest section of the town
It's out of place; looks somewhat crazed
Lopsided, "Where's the clown?"

On Friday night with boredom skipping steady in our room
We go for entertainment gay and sure
Prepared to witness backwoods' cripples swoon
And watch the gawdy faces pray for cure.

The hat is passed and poor men give their dollar
We laugh, guffaw, and jingle coins in jest
Someone says "pass it on" with a friendly holler
Or "just give the money, you have paid for less

Than to sneer at these proud people and their Christ;
Just go and know you've yet to pay the price."

Catholic Childhood

When I was but a child, a little one
And most impressionable at that early age
My mother wasn't well, I lived with nuns
And all the kids had said their heads were shaved.

To Jesus they all willingly gave their hair
When they all dressed in white had married him
They were such lovely virgins, all were fair
(I'd always thought that bigamy was a sin).

At Rosary they were menacing at their best
Without mistake their fingers read the beads
Each one they swore the Pope himself had blessed.
And I at Mass on Sundays on my knees

In the incensed chapel thick with hazy mood
I tasted the communion wafer-like fish food;
My wooden seat was waiting as my head in prayer was hung
And the wafer melted slowly, without meaning, on my
tongue.

Night and Morning

The lioness, amber dusk,
covers my fading room with her body.
The stars strike out too soon,
and I imagine them as mighty
gods of yore.

No blue roses grow before my eyes,
the calendar won't retract.
My dancing bears have danced to death,
Apollo won't come back.

And I lie under God, a funnel of darkness
from his breast to mine, feeling peace in
His silence, feeling peace in the emptiness
of night.

Breathing death through all my dreams, I wake,
still incognito.
The instruments of my solitary night are
painted now in melon.

And what the endless day to bring?
Where is my God of silence?
Who will help us fashion meaning?
Who will stand beside us?

Then I draw the lavender curtains
and dust the poetry of all my yesterdays.
So carefully must I handle this pain.

I Watched My Younger Sister

I watched my younger sister grow up
ahead of me;
She married her childhood sweetheart
and I was left to dream

quietly and alone
amid my tender walls of fantasy.

I saw the Virgin Mary in a vision
one day...
She spoke to me of sainthood and
blessed my purity.

And one night in vivid dreams
on a pale horse in grasses green
rode Einstein...
and he spoke to me of infinity.

Infinity, I laughed at him,
is for fools who live to win, the
years raffled off in coffee tins,
by false gods singing gypsy hymns

Then, when I thought my dreams were
done,
I met a man who said he'd come
to show me the ways of death were sweet
and looking into his deep blue eyes...
I followed him.

302

That morning
I woke up smiling.

Poets & Sad Cafés

Carson McCullers
Where are you?
Where is your sad café
                    coffee shop
                    café au lait

Edna St. Vincent Millay
Where are you?
Where is your sad café
                    friend that strayed
                    man who slayed

Jesus Christ
Where are you?
Where is your sad café
                    friend betrayed
                    man who stayed.

I Carry My Sins

I carry my sins
like a basket of
ripe strawberries
balanced wearily upon my head
fresh and ripe they are
tempting to spill again for supper

A small scented sin
textured as our loving
plumped for night-falls
spuriously as kisses fall
from my mouth to yours,
tumbling carelessly,
as if my basket were
a horn of plenty,
as if sins grew
easily as spring fruit.

If He Loves Us Why?

Where were you, God,
the day 51 men fell to their
deaths
    from a weak scaffold?

You're probably thinking:
    "I gave those bastards
a native intelligence.
    Dammed idiots!

It's not _my_ fault if
they refused to bring
their equipment up to code

It's not _my_ fault if
the blee----ping
rope broke!"

Nun's Story

I want to be a nun.
Sit with my hair shorn like a man's
in the cool marble chapel.
I will not know my body. My skin
will serve its own purpose only.

I will seek no pleasure I do not find.
Trees green willows will be my only dream.

I will be the blade of grass growing most
anonymously in a rosary of spring.
I will bear no children
nor know the male pain most women crave.
I will marry prayer; renounce ego.

I will live in a white cell with my white
heart and wooden chair.
Walnut colored beads will fall from my
waist and announce my coming with a
crucifix.

Flat on my face
I will marry away my past
with
one
cool
kiss.

Oh My Christ

Oh my Christ on that far-away cross
conjured up now on four-bit posters
and embossed
on bumper stickers.

Oh my Christ– super star of the 70's
and invisible healer of believers–
did you know you've made it big on Broadway
and are seen in Saturday night movie theaters?

This come-back, Jesus, I hope you realize I know
is not your second-coming.
Don't imagine that because you are popular now
and fattening the pockets of the Industry
that I know you any better.

Oh my Christ on that far-away cross–
every once in a while
I close my eyes and cry because I know I am not saved.
you spoke so long ago
your echo is only red letters now in a book I keep closed.
　　　　Not because I want to…
But because I think maybe you wouldn't like me.

Future

Oh God
As I kneel at the foot of this bare
Mountain
I see as my future
I need your strength within me
To rise like a rope to pull me up.

My hands have lost their grip,
My footfall is heavy and uncertain
And I thirst. But I cannot turn back
I cannot turn back and start again.
No one can.

This impasse is heavy within me
Like a rock
In the belly of a small bird.
I would sing praises to you
and be thankful
But my voice is mute;
My thanks false.

My limbs have worn from strength
To weakness
Yet I must climb
For there is no going back.

As I kneel at the foot of this bare
Mountain
I would ask your forgiveness

If only I could be sure
Of what I've done wrong.

Light is fading from the
Comforting arm of your sky
And...
If you are not there watching
Then I am alone.
A pinprick in a universe of
neverending stars and galaxies.

Yet, I cry out
Like a coyote calling out the moon.
Dumb.

Yet I will kneel a little longer
in homage
but soon I must rise
For your Voice
I thought I heard your Voice
Calling, calling
From the other side.

Prayer for Barmaids

I say a prayer for barmaids
and whistle under glass.
My boats have burst their bottles,
My sheep aren't coming home.
The Snow Queen died of cancer
from smoking far too long.

Now, flying swan,
you're leaving the scattered
Coke-bottle fair,
& me with my sadness
with cotton-candy in my hair.

Diet

My stomach unthaws and I
worry about over-eating
Not being sad enough to abstain,
and knowing
if sadness were decisive
I would starve.

Continuance

The water's cool liquidity
upon my breast did freely flow
and every love I ever knew
did bear upon my heart to show

that loves like water never go
but merge together
ever slow

and form one's soul
from sun to moon
into a sad continuance.

I Practice at Yoga

I practice at Yoga
and other heart-escaping
disciplines
but there is no escape
from heart.

Moon crescents curl messages
down from dark.

My heart dark, darkens.

Rainy Day Bus Ride

Let them want me
and not have me
It's about time
the shoe was on
the other foot.

Today...
The bus windshield wipers
are just a metronome
of despair.

The skies are leaden
concrete gray
Even when the bus rounds Greenlake
It isn't there....
Just another colorless pond
in the rain.

Streetlight-red radiates
its incandescent reflection
yard upon yard
of wet asphalt

diamond black.

Let them have me
and not want me.
I'm tired of looking back.

Backache

The ache in my back is
travelling like a junk
moving up the long, slow river of my spine.

A "Jack-in-the-Beanstalk" giant
pulls my muscles like taffy:
A heavy twist to the left;
A heavy twist to the right.
(to what rough hands must my body resign).

So, set the needles,
set the arrows,
you huntsmen and physicians,

And dam this long, slow river of pain
and set me
free again.

Infidelity

I search for a weapon to arm myself with.

In the long interlude between your confession
and my regret...

I search for a weapon to injure;
not kill
there's nothing fatal
about the way I feel.

I search for a weapon to wound;
not ruin,
It's hard to forgive another woman.

and I'm sure in her rented room
waiting by a waiting phone
she searches,
spends her time searching for
a weapon too.

Do Not Doubt Me Now

Do not doubt me now
now between the flowers and the grace;
between the spacious
certainty that
all will be forgiven
and the lie.

Do not doubt me now
now between the shadow and the smile;
between the hallelujahs
and the long goodbye.

Do not doubt me now
now between the garden and the frost
between the knowing
and a lost solemity.

Do not doubt me now
now between the kitchen and the bath;
between the naked lunch
and the paragraph
between a poem unwritten
and the raven's song;
Do not doubt this right
or the myopic wrongs

Walking the Dog

Across from the library
I spot him
circling the phone booth
wearing a 20-year old forest green
Pendleton jacket.

Cars on Greenwood zip by in anonymous blur
and it's trying to rain.

His feet shuffle the ground; marry the
damp concrete.
His thumbs, I suppose, seek the holes in his
pockets like blind worms wiggling toward
the light.

I've seen him before
while taking the evening air
with my good husband... have seen his little dog;
the bedraggled leash; the love they wore.

But now I sense these are the eyes of a lonesome
drinker. I can almost count the rooms he's rented
by the circles of pain haunting his red eyes.

A wife perhaps?
Gone.
Or children he never had
manifest by the silent phone.

We play ring-round-the rosey round the flyer-stapled
telephone pole.
See...
there's no dog.
no leash.

Could it be he's on his own
with that tiny death all the love he'll ever know.

Farewell

When coming down the unlit stair
Going to a place you know
Is green and cold
You turn around for a brief,
Last moment
And see me; a small smile,
A goodbye gown.

Remember,
That the love I gave to you
Is yours to keep
And I will follow in a year or two.